Our Favorite Sonoma Stories

From Wine Country in Shorts

Ralph De Amicis & Lahni De Amicis

Cuore Libre Publishing
Napa California

Our Favorite Sonoma Stories
From Wine Country in Shorts
By Ralph & Lahni De Amicis

Published by Cuore Libre Publishing
Napa, California
www.WineCountryInShortscom

Copyright 2025 Ralph & Lahni De Amicis
ISBN 979-8-3485-9922-5
No part of this book may be reproduced in any form without permission from the publisher.

Maps: Ralph De Amicis
Photos Lahni DeAmicis & Ralph DeAmicis

Pg 16. San Carolos entering San Francisco Bay by By Walter Francis - Public Domain

Contents

Introduction: A Land of Stories 5

Chapter 1: The Mysterious Golden Gate 11

Chapter 2: The Gift of Mustard 25

Chapter 3: Thoroughly Cool Los Carneros 35

Chapter 4: They All Came to Sonoma 49

Chapter 5: The Magical Valley of the Moon 63

Chapter 6: The Imperial Russian River Story 71

Chapter 7: Wine Country's Great Buildings 79

Chapter 8: Sonoma and Napa; Ancient Siblings 107

Chapter 9: Who Named Mount Saint Helena? 119

Afterthought, the Fans 133

About the Authors 137

Other Books & Documentaries 138

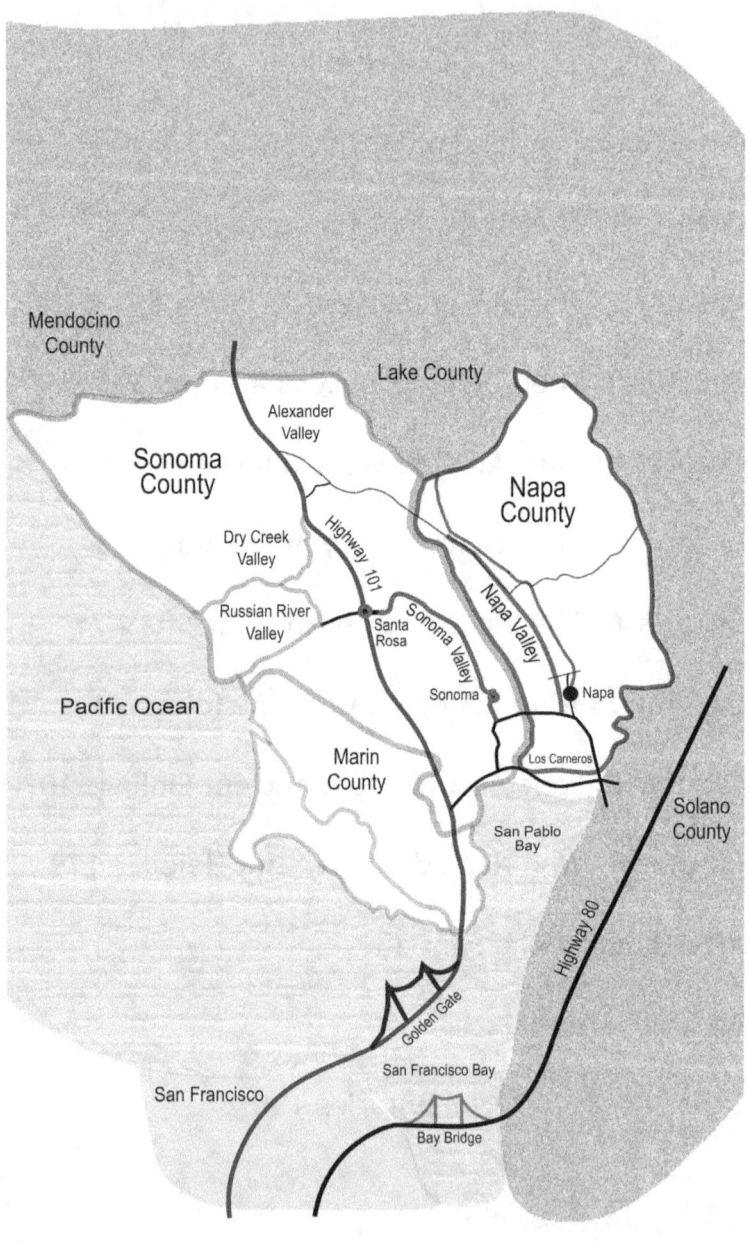

Introduction: A Land of Stories

This book celebrates the unique storytelling style that goes well with wine: colorful, relaxed, thoughtful, a little rambling and segmented. That's because the pace of the story allows time for the listeners to taste the wines and enjoy the illumination it bestows. That's how the ancients described the experience of drinking alcohol, being illuminated by the wine.' We hope that you enjoy these stories that are only as remarkable as the wonderful places and people they describe, and that are treasured by so many.

    A wine region's personality is not just about the topography and climate, but also about how the people living there adapted to its unique qualities. Those experiences are shared in stories. Where did we get these stories? We heard them while standing at the back of countless tasting rooms. For many years there were a couple of hundred wineries where customers could just walk in, stand at the bar and taste the wines. At other wineries the tastings happened sitting down, and of course there are cave and vineyard tours. In these tasting experiences, the hosts shared information about the wines, and many shared stories.

In any given year we visited over three hundred tasting rooms, and we heard so many stories, and multiple versions of those stories! The overall feeling was very casual, relaxed and friendly.

We retold these stories countless times to groups and wine tour clients while driving around the North Bay Wine Country. It was easy to recall those tales when we visited those places where the events occurred. So, to pull together the stories for this book, Ralph started dictating the, into his phone while our clients were tasting at the wineries. We wanted to write down these stories for a while, but it was hard to find the time. And then a fortuitous thing happened. The local wine tasting fees escalated, and the wineries recognized that if they abandoned their quick tasting bars, in favor of longer seated experiences, their sales would improve.

Honestly, any tour guide could have told them that! The big wines grown in the Napa vineyards taste better when you give them time to open up in the glass. However, as the tastings became more formal, exclusive and expensive, it was a rare time when we stayed with our clients during the sessions.

That scheduling change suddenly gave Ralph a predictable amount of precious, uninterrupted time to dictate the stories, and then later improve the drafts. Choosing the stories was hard becuase an amazing number pop out of his mouth as he drives around with clients. Sometimes he remembers a story because they are passing the winery where a friend first shared it with him.

Many stories have been around so long that there are multiple published versions. For instance, four different people from three groups are credited with naming Mount Saint Helena, the beautiful volcanic cone that towers over the northern valleys.

But, if you keep an open mind, dig deep enough into the research, and account for human nature, you can weave the various versions together into an enjoyable, credible narrative that's pretty close to the truth.

For us, this reweaving happened spontaneously through telling the stories numerous times while noticing both our listeners responses, and whether or not it 'felt' true as we spoke the words. That is a concept from the healing arts, because hearing lies makes us weaker, while hearing the truth makes us stronger!

On the road we've shared these tales with clients in 15 to 20-minute snippets, which is the ideal driving time between wineries, because it allows enough time to metabolize some of the alcohol in preparation for another tasting. But here we've combined those pieces into complete stories, and many turned out to be much longer than we expected.

Even though the stories give us the narrative, in the full version of Wine Country in Shorts, and in our book, A Tour Guide's series of books, we describe the traditions and practices in the winemaking world. These seem to be endlessly interesting to our clients, but that's not surprising.

Two hundred years ago most people worked on the land. Today a tiny fraction of Americans grows everyone else's food and wine, so for most people, this life on the land is far removed from their personal universe. But there must be some deep region within us that still yearns for that ancestral connection to nature.

Is it due to our ancestry, our genetics, or simply our sensual enjoyment of wine, that so many people are drawn to visit the places where it's made? We think the answer to that is 'Yes,' to all of the above! Winemaking is a very elegant type of agriculture that has delightful results.

Visiting this region is an adventure, although not as risky as it was in the early 1800's when visitors had to contend with the numerous California grizzly bears that lived here. There were so many that outside the region the word Napa meant Bear, and the mountains that separated the two counties was a favorite home for these alpha predators. We think that's why bravery and audacity are so prized locally, and why the region attracts so many of the big personalities who show up in these stories from the past and present.

We're sure a scientific study would show that wine tastes better when accompanied by a story, and any story becomes more enjoyable when the wine is good.

Any experienced winery host knows that's true, which is why, as they fill the glasses, the best share stories about the winery's history and location. There's only so much you can say about what's in the glass, because to our bodies, flavor is a language, and great wines have no problem speaking for themselves.

When they tell the story of the struggles involved in clearing the land, planting the vines, building the winery and making a good wine, that connects the guest to that bottle in an emotionally memorable way. Later, when the guest opens the bottle at home, that memory makes the wine taste 'better,' and they have the added pleasure of telling that story to their friends and family.

So, we feel that the best way to enjoy these stories is with a glass of wine in your hand. If you are listening to this as an audio book while driving in a car, we'll give you a pass on that.

Lahni's Editor Note: The Northern California Wine Country is peppered with similar and overlapping stories, many from slightly different perspectives, so you will find that some of the details are repeated, often with a twist that reveals a bit more about the bigger story. So, feel free to dip into the book at any chapter and know that the repetition is intentional, and you will also be better prepared for the Quiz at the end of the book. ***(Just kidding, or are we?)***

The Historic Toscana Hotel, Sonoma Plaza
Opposite: Golden Gate looking Southwest

Chapter One
The Mysterious Golden Gate

For visitors coming to California who are trying to understand its unique nature, it helps to realize that Spain and Mexico controlled a string of influential settlements in this expansive region for hundreds of years. That explains its laid-back nature, especially in the southern part where Spain reigned the longest. *Northern California is different.* When you cross the Golden Gate Bridge from San Francisco and drive towards Sonoma County, you're venturing into the northern tip of where the Spanish empire once stretched in the Americas.

During that early colonial period, Spain was a major power and their territories included Florida, half of south America, Central America, Mexico and the

American southwest. Eventually, they reached this far north but no further, leaving a trail of towns with Spanish names; San Diego, Los Angeles, Santa Barbara, Santa Cruz and pretty much 'Saint Everybody Else.' They completed their city naming spree at the top of the Sonoma Valley with a city named for the first Saint from the Americas, Santa Rosa de Lima.

The road that connected their California Missions together was *the 'Camino Real,' or 'Royal Road.'* It wound north from Guatemala, then to Mexico City through the rugged interior. It follows ancient Aztec and Rio Grande Pueblo tribal foot trails to New Mexico, and then west to the Pacific Coast. There the Franciscans established the first California Mission named for 'San Diego' and over the years worked their way north. El Camino Royal was the original Main Street in many California towns, including the little city of Sonoma, *where it ends at their Plaza* and the final Franciscan Mission, 'San Francisco Solano.'

In California the ancient road has been marked with a series of bells on top of shepherd's crooks. Being the site of one of the twenty-one missions is the gold standard for qualification as an historic site. The second tier goes to the Spanish forts, or Presidios for which San Francisco's famous army base was named.

Finally, the third criterion belongs to the six Spanish Pueblos, the cities where courts were convened, and official records kept. The surprisingly small city of *Sonoma is the only place in California that enjoyed all three of these distinctions*, albeit for the shortest period of time.

But I'm getting ahead of myself, so let's go back to where so much of the North Bay's story begins, the Golden Gate Pass at the entrance to the San Francisco Bay. It sits midway up the coast of California, and *it's cunningly hidden from the seaward side.* Since the mid-fifteen hundreds Spanish galleons had sailed past the strait unaware, on the way back from their bases in the Philippines six thousand sea miles to the west.

After a five-month journey returning from the spice islands, they would make landfall along the Northern California coast. After taking on fresh water, and whatever other supplies they could find, they would turn south towards their base in Acapulco. *They sailed well off the coast* to avoid the submerged dangers along the rocky shore. They named their various landings along the coast including Point Mendocino, Bodega Bay and Tomales Bay.

Western historians often neglect to mention that the Portuguese and Spanish first successfully ventured into those distant seas *using charts created by Chinese cartographers* who had come before them. In the early 1400's, during the Ming Dynasty, the Yongle Emperor dispatched seven fleets of Chinese 'Treasure ships' to map the world. Those grand ships were *twice the size* of the largest Spanish Galleons, and they were accompanied by smaller Korean and Japanese trading vessels.

Fortunately for the Spanish, one of the fleets meticulously mapped the Pacific coastlines of North and south America, including Magellan's passage, which provided easier access between the Atlantic and the Pacific Oceans. They also mapped what we know today as the San Francisco Bay.

However, when ships sail into unknown waters there are always shipwrecks, which explains why early Spanish explorers *reported seeing Chinese junks sailing along the coast in the 1500's*. The Spanish sailors recognized the design of the Chinese trading junks from their travels in the Western Pacific and the Indian Ocean. There were so many sightings that the Spanish concluded that there must be a Chinese city nearby. They called this place they never found *Quivira*, after Francisco Vasquez de Coronado's 'Seven Cities of Gold.'

Even though it is possible that those ships were recent arrivals, more than likely, they were repaired and sailed by the shipwrights and sailors that had been left behind when the fleet sailed home in the mid-1400's. That's not surprising, because unlike European ships, the Chinese crews included both men and women, so between shipwrecks and the inevitable babies, there were more people in the fleet than berths on the remaining ships.

There is plenty of genetic evidence that Chinese communities from the fleets remained behind in the Americas. As they watched the ships sail away, they surely expected them to return. *Sorry!* By the time the fleets made home port the Yongle Emperor had died. His xenophobic son, appalled at the massive expense of the fleets, systematically closed the borders and put an end to their mapping and exploring. The new Emperor and the influential Mandarins closed China off from the rest of the world for the next four hundred years. *As an interesting footnote* of that decision, a California State anthropologist found a village of 'Indians' in the Russian River Valley in the 1800s *who only spoke Chinese*. The next time a Chinese ship would enter the Golden Gate Pass was in 1850, bringing immigrants into San Francisco Harbor.

Even though the Chinese withdrew into their 'Middle Kingdom,' they left behind the world maps created by their fleet cartographers in places like Kolkata (Calcutta), a trading port the Chinese had established in earlier sea going days on the coast of India. It was there that Venetian navigators found the charts and brought them home to 'La Serenissima,' their beloved Venice. The charts helped Venice expand into a major sea power.

Their rise did not go unnoticed and led to a heavily disguised Prince Henry of Portugal smuggling the charts out of Venice to the Iberian Peninsula. Those precious charts were the keys to prosperity for his country, and if he had been caught, he would not have survived. Henry set up a sailing school on the Portugeuse coast to train crews to use those maps.

Today, on its site, a statue of *'Prince Henry the Navigator'* looks out over the ocean. With the help of the Chinese charts, he developed a sea route to the spice islands. They avoided the dangerous Venetians and Arabians, by going around the tip of Africa. In a shockingly brief period of time Portugal went from being Europe's poorest country to its wealthiest.

Eventually, the Spanish and English, through captured ships, obtained those charts, and Magellan used one to find his passage to the Pacific. Sir Francis Drake depended on them *when he circumnavigated the globe* in the late 1570's, landing north of modern San Francisco, on a section of coastline that he claimed for England. This was a serious puzzle for Captain Drake because the Chinese charts showed a great bay along this part of the coast. The Spanish had sailed these shores for years but failed to find its location. Drake surely wanted to claim that prize for himself as it would make his fortune. But just because the chart said it was there, that didn't make it easy to find.

The Spanish Ship San Carolos

From our perspective today it's hard to imagine what those navigators contended with. We are accustomed to seeing the shoreline from the decks of cruise ships, a hundred feet above the water, or looking down at where the land meets the water while flying above the Earth in airplanes. During Drake's time, the first flights of the Wright Brothers were hundreds of years in the future. What you could see from the low deck of a bobbing ship, was what you knew. While the San Francisco Bay is expansive, its sole opening to the sea is a narrow strait, barely a mile wide *and it hides in plain sight*. At the time when Drake was tramping along the coast, impenetrable marshlands lined much of the shoreline that fronted steep cliffs.

For a sailor looking eastward from the sea the view is deceptive, because beyond that narrow opening are both Alcatraz Island, one of modern San Francisco's most popular destinations, and Angel Island, the *'Ellis Island of the west.'* Then beyond those two grassy mounts are the green hills of Berkeley. Their various heights conspire to make the pass appear as a solid wall of rocks and vegetation meeting the churning sea.

Then to complicate a ship pilot's life, there are the famous fog banks that blanket the area for many months of the year, making the coastline appear and disappear like a magician's rabbit. As if that wasn't enough to dissuade mariners from venturing closer, California's two largest rivers empty into the ocean through the Golden Gate. The turbulence that pours out of that narrow opening is epic, filled with whirlpools and eddies that can swallow a small boat.

The only reason there aren't more wrecks sitting on the bottom surrounding the harbor, like we see at ports around the world, is because so few ships could find their way there in the first place. Because those two rivers carry nutrients from magnificently fertile countryside, the waters offshore are packed with life. That makes the shallows around the nearby Farallon Islands the perfect breeding ground for one of the ocean's great alpha predators, the absolutely *terrifying great white shark*.

So, let's see if we've got this straight. When the sailors passed that part of the rocky coast in their little wooden ships, what they saw was *fog enshrouded, tumultuous, shark infested waters* that any smart, experienced Captain would avoid. It's amazing that the Chinese found the entrance in the 1400's, and we know that they did because there's wreckage from their ebony ships buried under the silt of the Sacramento River a hundred miles upstream.

When the Spanish arrived at the Sacramento Delta in the 1700's, the local 'Indians' were farming rice in those fertile lowlands, a plant that traces its origins to the banks of China's Yangtze River, now known as the Chang Jiang. Even today, you can see the squat and ridiculously cute rice silos dotting the local fields. The advantage that the Chinese cartographers enjoyed aboard their spacious ships were stables for horses. They could easily ride along the coast with their instruments, taking their sightings and making their notations.

The Golden Gate could not stay hidden forever from the European navigators once they had the Chinese charts, *but still it eluded them from the seaward side.* How did they find it? The story has been told for generations by the Bay Area families of the twenty-one Spanish soldiers who walked thirty miles north from Half Moon Bay and practically fell into the watery inlet. The Franciscan monk in charge had ordered them to reach Point Reyes, a pointy spit of beach, jutting out into the ocean thirty miles north of the Golden Gate Pass. That's *where Drake had landed two hundred years before* and curiously, Point Reyes sits right on the troublesome San Andreas fault line where two tectonic plates come together.

The party made their way north and came to the wall of marshlands that once ringed the bay. So, they headed inland, probably because the coastal route was so cold. As they traveled inland, they encountered a violent band of braves that *aggressively charged their party,* keeping up their attacks until the soldiers fearfully turned back. Hoping for a safer route, the party walked towards the coast and up the peninsula into what is today modern San Francisco.

They were making satisfactory progress until their way was blocked by the tumultuous, deep waters of an inlet. Being soldiers and not sailors *they deemed the route to Point Reyes impassable without a boat.* As simple soldiers they had never seen the Chinese charts drawn three centuries before. Such things were only for trusted navigators.

They didn't realize *they had just discovered* the entrance to one of the world's great bays, something that had evaded European explorers for two centuries. Feeling defeated at not reaching their destination, they returned to Half Moon Bay. They apologetically explained to the Franciscan Monk how they failed to reach their destination, due to the marshes, the devilish Indians and the 'unexpected body of water that touched the sea.'

Despite the significance of their find, it was several more years before enough of the threads were pulled together that the Spanish navigators could match the shoreline from the Chinese charts with the reports of this expedition. Finally, in 1775, the unlikely Spanish supply ship, 'San Carolos', with a *young, inexperienced Captain,* found the entrance to the harbor. He had been promoted at the last minute because his Captain went crazy just before weighing anchor at Monterey. Possibly his youth led him to be more daring and willing to venture where the previous captains had feared to tread.

First, he cautiously sent a rowboat though the pass. When his mate reported back that it was clear they sailed the ship through the treacherous waters, finally mooring off Angel Island in Ayala Cove, *named for the courageous young Captain.* It's located just below a steep slice of land called Tiburon, which not surprisingly means 'shark.' Obviously, the sleek gray predators that patrolled the strait's entrance impressed them.

That was before freighters and steel warships plied these waters and encouraged the natural world to give them a wider berth. Over the next two months, the pilots used the longboats to map the bay's expanse. Captain Ayala and his men befriended the mostly naked local tribes, who envied their warm coats. Even though they marveled at this amazing discovery, they had yet to see the Eden-like valleys to the north.

It's accepted that the favorite place to moor boats is along the steep Sausalito shore, where you'll find all shapes and sizes of craft, including *the town's eccentric and colorful houseboats.* The town's location on the leeward side of the Marin headlands shields it from the cool Pacific breezes, so when the fog wraps around the headlands, it leaves a patch of blue sky above the town. Many a time I have sat in the local cafés, sipping a coffee while watching the fog flow between the high-rises across the bay.

While the Chinese Treasure fleets were long gone by the time the Spanish appeared along the coast, *many other countries have raised their flags over California.* The stickiest problem was Sir Francis Drake's claim. The Spanish clearly controlled the area south of the bay, with a prominent Presidio in Monterey. That's where the future commandant of Sonoma, Mariano Guadalupe Vallejo was born.

Even though it was years since Drake had raised the English flag over Point Reyes and Bodega Bay, *the English had never relinquished the claim,* and that posed a problem for the Russian Governor of Alaska. He needed a warm coastal settlement where his people could grow food to support his fishing bases.

The Russian Governor was wary of infringing on the powerful and quite testy Spanish, so he consulted with their leader. he felt he could conveniently ignore Drake's previous claim, because this was the ends of the Earth. So, he sent a ship south to establish what is commonly called Fort Ross. Although pronounced 'Fort Ross,' it was named for 'Mat' Rossiya,' or Mother Russia. Their settlement was just north of where the shoal choked Russian River empties into the Pacific, and it gave them a warm, fertile place to farm and raise animals. In a delicate bit of diplomacy, they avoided the lovely natural harbor at

Bodega Bay, claimed by Drake, but named by the Spanish. Instead, they chose a spot along the steep, wooded coast just north of the *unnavigable Russian River,* because no other seagoing power would be interested in wrenching such a marginal ship's landing from their grip.

The success of this settlement caused some serious stress for the Spanish who had Presidios in Monterey and on the shores of the San Francisco Bay. In an aggressive geopolitical chess move, now Lieutenant Vallejo was sent from Monterey to establish *a Presidio north of the bay and closer to the Russians.*

The spot he chose became the little city of Sonoma, the most historic place in California. His mandate was to prevent the 'Russian Bear's' influence from spreading to the south, which was a problem because *the Russians were well-liked by the locals.* Also, Vallejo was a genial man who was happy to have a good relationship with them and really didn't have enough soldiers to make it an issue.

Eventually, when the Americans arrived in greater numbers, the Russians abandoned their 'fort,' it had cannons but no soldiers. The Czar was afraid that his people would become *'infected with democracy.'* So yes, it was good old Russian paranoia that made them leave Paradise, although not all of them did.

There are still old Russian families in that part of the Redwood Empire, as it's traditionally known, and in San Francisco, once again, thanks to the Golden Gate. After the Czar of Russia fell from power, aristocrats fled the country, and a favorite route was from their westernmost port, Vladivostok, to the Golden Gate and San Francisco. Not surprisingly, *they settled in an area called 'Russian Hill.'* This steep, picturesque neighborhood was named for an early colonial cemetery, the final resting place for Russian fur trappers who were hunting the precious sea otters, and occasionally coming to an unfortunate end.

The Russian Aristocrats were an entirely different breed from the early trappers because they arrived with their gold and jewelry, which they put in the city's banks. The story goes that so much wealth left 'Mother Rossiya' in those émigré's trunks, that the Russians paid informants working in the oldest banks. They were to watch for members of the old Russian families accessing their safe deposit boxes from that period. This commercial espionage went on until the fall of the Soviet Union.

The Golden Gate has consistently been the source of the city's wealth. At the time of the Gold Rush, thousands of miners arrived on their way to the Sierra Madres. Then t*he gold flowed* through those banks and back out the Gate on ships. Even that didn't compare to the wealth from the Nevada silver mines which arrived in the city's banks and firmly established it as a financial powerhouse. All of this prosperity is in addition to the vast amount of agricultural wealth that passes through the Gate, *and not just from the wine.*

Which brings us back around to poor Sir Francis Drake. He had unknowingly suffered a bit of bad luck. *For the lack of a good walk* of about ten miles down the coast from Point Reyes, he missed finding the entrance to the San Francisco Bay. With its great natural harbors and navigable rivers, it is the envy of the world. If Drake returned today, from his landfall at Point Reyes, he could ride east on Sir Francis Drake Boulevard to Route 101, once called the Redwood Highway. Then he could follow 101 south over the Golden Gate Bridge to San Francisco's Union Square.

After an appreciative glance at the statue of the beautiful Uma Spreckels, high atop her towering podium, he could march into the Sir Francis Drake Hotel and demand a suite. I'm sure they would be happy to accommodate him, since they owe him a small fortune in royalties for using his name for so many years.

Admittedly, there has been talk of renaming that boulevard, because while his ships sailed under the English Flag, the Jolly Roger would have been equally appropriate. We must remember that sailors once compared this part of the coastline to the pirate infested Barbary Coast of Africa, so Drake would feel right at home as he looked out from his suite over the busy square, *as he raided the minibar. Argh!*

Chapter Two
The Gift of Mustard

Most visitors come to Wine Country in the warmer weather, with peak season happening during harvest in the late Summer through early Fall. It's a festive time of year when the vines are heavy with fruit and the scent of crushed grapes fills the air. We often explain to clients that they'll rarely see grapes being picked because that normally takes place in the coolness of night, under tractor mounted lights, for the sake of both the grape's freshness and the worker's comfort. But, if they're up and out early, they'll see the fruit laden trucks arriving at the crush pads at dawn, when the winemakers take over.

Fewer people visit during the cooler off-season. They're mostly the Canadian snowbirds and collectors, who are anxious to taste the vintages released in the

Spring, and happy for fewer tourists on the roads and in the wineries. At that time of year, the vines are dormant, the bushy canopies of leaves have been blown away by the Winter winds, and the workers are pruning away last year's canes. The *vineyards are transformed* into tight rows of woody vines, revealing their simple, orderly geometry. But the visitors are rewarded for their off-season travel with a delightful floral display. Bright yellow bands of wild mustard flowers appear like magic carpet runners, laid down between the bare grapevines. The yellow blooms add a touch of sunshine to the vineyards during our Winter rainy season.

They are a unique signature of Winter in the North Bay Wine Country when the rains transform the bleached, golden hillsides to a verdant green, making it the favorite season for many locals. While many trees keep their leaves, the deciduous trees go bare making the statuesque evergreens stand out. As the views open up they offer peeks of the spectacular hillside homes and wineries that are normally hidden by Summer's leafy privacy screens.

I've often joked that in Summer this region looks like *Tuscany* while in Winter, it looks like *Ireland*, if only the Irish grew grapes instead of shamrocks. Of course, with climate change, the way the English are currently growing sparkling wine grapes, it's less of a joke than I once thought. What's remarkable for people from outside the area is how quickly the look of the place changes. From the moment when the first rains arrive, a lush groundcover springs up between the bare vines. You can practically watch it grow, and very quickly it's followed by the tiny yellow mustard flowers, appearing like stars emerging from a darkening sky.

But *Wine Country is farm country*, albeit with great restaurants, so the cover crops the vintners choose for the wet Winter hiatus depends upon the needs of the land. A primary consideration is helping the bare ground stand up to Winter's wind and rain. It's important to keep the dirt securely in place around the roots to discourage both disease and industrious gophers. Next the choice depends on what nutrients the vines need. If they have a hankering for nitrogen, they may plant some type of bean, to capture that element from the air and bind it into its roots.

When the springtime plow comes through, the mineral will be released into the soil by the blades. Once or twice, I've seen vineyards with stripes of red clover flowers, but that deep pink bud is more commonly used as a cover for other crops. Mustard and wild radish's talent for inhibiting problematic insects makes them a popular choices.

Ground covers also serve other purposes. When a vineyard finally runs out of steam and the vines are ripped out, the vintners will begin the lengthy process of preparing the land for the new vines. If they want to lighten heavy clay soil, they'll plant the herb, borage. I've often seen those tall spindles reaching up from recently cleared ground near the river, aware that they are digging even more deeply into the clay. Just once I saw a fallow vineyard *planted with spectacular sunflowers,* but that was a special time. The longtime owner of the vineyard, a native of Kansas, had passed away so the family had planted that state's official flower in a glorious tribute for everyone to see.

Not surprisingly, the farmers are happy when a helpful groundcover comes up by itself with the rain, saving them the work and expense of planting. That's one of the talents of the very prolific wild mustard, making it the area's most popular Winter cover. We often see it growing wild by the side of the road and in abandoned meadows. But often, farmers plant it in time for the Winter rains because it's rich in phosphorus, which gives grapes a strong, thick skin, and produces spectacular colors in the wine.

Flavors live in the skin and the more they can encourage that healthy layer with bright sunshine, the tastier the resulting wines will be. That's why you'll see workers removing the leaves that are shading the bunches but leaving the ones on the other side that protect them from the wind.

The wild mustard flowers are so widespread in the North Bay Wine Country that locals watch for their annual appearance and passing as an indicator of the changing seasons. At the peak of its season, it's common to see lines of cars on the weekend pulled up alongside especially abundant fields, as visitors stream out with their cameras to capture that brilliance. The blooming mustard is so much a part of our daily lives that most people would be surprised to find out that *it's not a native plant,* quite the contrary.

Even though mustard plants are found throughout the world, the bright little yellow flowers were first brought here by the Franciscan Monks in the 1800s. Historically, trailblazers always carried items for trade, because there's nothing like exotic gifts to open the doors of potentially unfriendly locals, like the beads and bangles infamously used to purchase Manhattan.

Mustard is a valuable plant, for both its medicinal and culinary qualities. The pungent flavors must have been *a wonderful surprise* to the native people and its ability to stimulate healing warmth and sweats could be lifesaving.

Today it's hard to imagine the world that these explorers were walking into, out there at the 'Ends of the Earth.' While they carried several wonderfully helpful items, the sad reality is that the most prized trading items were sharpened steel weapons and tools. They were a valuable and unknown resource in pre-colonial America. The Franciscans *used those as bribes* for recruiting the native people, sending steel armed allies to kidnap the children of other tribes for converts and slaves.

One of their most famous 'converts' was Chief Solano, who had been stolen from the Suisun tribe, *'the people of the wind,'* to be raised at the Sonoma Mission. He grew into a towering, powerful brave taking for his Christian name the namesake of the mission, Saint Francisco Solano, a Spanish missionary to Peru. The Chief became an important ally and friend of General Vallejo, the military commander of all Spanish, and then later Mexican possessions north of the Bay.

But the native people were not of one mind, and not every tactic worked every time. One tribe that *resolutely resisted the missionaries* and their soldiers was the Napa Wappo, who made their home in the upper valley. This was due to a combination of personality, geology and economics. They were called the 'Wappo', a misnomer from the Spanish word 'guapo' meaning 'handsome and brave,' but the people called themselves the 'Onasatis,' meaning the *'outspoken ones.'* They were a brave people, although their neighbors described them as warlike.

What was it about the Onasatis that made them less susceptible to the Spanish's offers of steel tools, since they could be a wonderful help in the arduous work of providing food and clothing? It's easy to forget that when the Europeans arrived in the Americas the native people *were using stone tools*. The 'Bronze Age' and the 'Iron Age' during which Europe and Asian had developed those technologies had completely bypassed the Americans.

The native people went right from living in the 'Stone Age' to using the technology of the 'Age of Exploration' when steel became widely available. Obviously, sharp tools are important in a hunter-gatherer community, but economically, this *new source of steel tools was competition* for the stone tools that the tribes were using! Where did the stone tools come from? The absolute best came from Napa.

Over the years, the Onasatis had gradually expanded to the south into the Napa Valley from their villages in Northern Sonoma, taking control of an area known today as Glass Mountain. Coincidentally, this is where the 2020 Napa fire began that burned forty percent of the county. In that area there's an abundance of volcanic glass chips that speckle the ground. This black *'obsidian'* is the sharpest material on the planet, capable of being sharpened to a single molecule, so even today it's used for the finest scalpels. Not surprisingly it makes sharpest arrowheads, knives, axes and tools. Several local wineries display the tribe's shredding boards.

These long, flat pieces of wood were embedded with hundreds of obsidian chips. They were used by the native people for turning the abundant acorns produced by the stately "valley oaks" into flour, a staple in their diet. The obsidian deposits made the Onasatis *an important part of a trading network* that spread throughout the Bay Area.

The valley's trading trail traveled from the base of Mount Saint Helena in the north, along the eastern hills, above the valley's flood plan, ending in the south at the first wide section of the river near what is today downtown Napa. It *became the basis* for today's Silverado Trail. If you follow the Napa River to the south from there you come to a narrow, watery strait that connects the Sacramento River to the San Pablo Bay, and from there, the San Francisco Bay.

Today that is the site of the Carquinez Bridge. That takes its name for the 'Carquin' tribe that made its home there. In Patwin, the word translates as 'traders,' because they ran the marketplace.

The Onasatis' command of this unique resource made the Spanish and their steel tools competition for this centuries old source of prosperity. The 'Outspoken Ones' ongoing resistance to the invaders ended with them being forcibly removed by the American Cavalry from their *'Talahalusi,' or 'beautiful land,'* to colder settlements on the distant Mendocino Coast. So, the world that the Spanish walked into was a complex culture and trading network they brutally disrupted in their search for gold and converts. But for now, let's leave that sad part of the story behind and get back to the curious story of the wild mustard.

There was another practical reason that the missionaries carried those heavy bags of mustard seeds. Even though the Franciscans had their faults, they were well trained, and it was their job to plot the path that became the Royal Road, *'El Camino Real.* Today the ancient route is marked by a line of shepherd's crooks with bells atop them alongside the highways. The road connected together the sites of California's original twenty-one Franciscan missions.

Following this well-trodden path, you could walk, or ride on horseback, from San Diego to Sonoma in twenty-one days, barring encounters with bears, wolves, rattlesnakes, mountain lions or any native warriors in a bad mood. While the Franciscans depended on the Spanish soldiers for protection, their scholarship and navigation skills made them valuable, albeit demanding leaders.

Today as we drive down our GPS mapped highways, we think of the little mustard seed's contribution to hot dogs and buns, but those Franciscan explorers put the mustard flowers to a clever use. The technique has its origins with the ancient Roman mapmakers, the Roman's loved spicy food and spread their favorite plants, grapes, olives and mustard, throughout their expansive empire!

Like the Romans, the Franciscans carried a bag of mustard seeds with a little hole in the bottom, so it would leave a trail of seeds behind them. In the Spring, when they emerged from their snug Winter quarters and retraced their steps, there would be *lines of the bright yellow flowers springing up*, showing them where they had traveled before. If they needed mustard seeds to spice a meal or compound a remedy, the plants were always handy. It is wonderful to realize that many of California's oldest roads started their lives as paths trimmed with beds of mustard flowers.

Today, the joyful eruption of brightness between the bare vines of Winter is the Franciscan's gift and it's an experience that the locals joyfully anticipate. It also makes our returning wintertime visitors *smile*, because it's a sign that they, like those hearty explorers, have arrived at what the Onasatis called their *'Talahalusi,'* their beautiful place.

Chapter Three
Thoroughly Cool Los Carneros

It makes no sense to name a wine region 'Los Carneros,' or 'the Rams,' but that's what the Spanish wrote on the 1820's land-grant that encompassed the rolling hills perched at the southern edge of the Napa and Sonoma Valleys. It's bordered on the south by the San Pablo Bay, an olive-shaped, shallow stretch of water that juts north of the San Francisco Bay. The Spanish couldn't imagine that this cool, windy region would someday produce world class wines. To them, it seemed *a good place to graze their woolly flocks.* Compared to the warmth of the Sonoma Plaza where the Spanish first settled, these hills seemed inhospitable to anyone except shepherds, who are accustomed to a rough life.

Since antiquity, the Ram, or Aries, has been the astrological sign that marks the beginning of Spring. That fits because Los Carneros enjoys a perpetual Spring. Most days are cool, dry, with bright sunshine followed by cold nights. The North Bay is *a place of extremes* and Los Carneros is at the forefront of that. One of the secrets of the North Bay's talent for growing wine grapes is the glassy surface of the San Pablo Bay. It acts as a mirror, casting the reflected sunshine to the north creating what The Weather Channel calls 'abundant sunshine'. The vineyards that sit closest to that mirror are in Los Carneros.

But the strength of the sunlight is not the only factor. At night, the cool fog rolls in from the bay, blanketing Los Carneros before traveling up the valleys like a misty river. In the morning, it withdraws south and eventually slips out through the Golden Gate, like a Genie returning to their bottle. That leaves the local vineyards shrouded in fog much longer than the northern valleys. As the morning sunshine grows stronger it travels through a refractive filter of water particles, creating *color-filled rainbows* that the wine grapes turn into micro-nutrients that we experience as flavors!

This is important wherever the fog travels, but it is most at home in Los Carneros and coincidentally, where they grow the same grape varietals as in the Russian River Valley, Chardonnay and Pinot Noir. This band of land along the bay is geologically different from the warmer valleys to the north. Under its rolling green hills lies an *ancient, basaltic seabed* which adds crispness to the wines. That's different from the volcanic ridges and iron rich riverbeds found in the upper valleys that promote great depth of flavors in the wines. The brightness encouraged by the basalt rich soil is one of the reasons that the sparkling wines have done so well here.

Then there's the wind! Every day, the Los Carneros wind comes in off the San Pablo Bay and soars over the hills like a great nature spirit. Grapevines are sensitive to wind and when it blows too strongly, the leaves close their pores to preserve their moisture and the vine stops making sugar. This short circuit in the growing cycle allows the thin-skinned grapes, like Pinot Noir, enough time to make the deeper flavors that people prize, without producing the excessive sugar that would turn into ballistic alcohol in the finished wine. While high alcohol sounds like fun, it's not graceful, the careful balancing of diverse components is at the heart of great winemaking.

Los Carneros is obviously unique in the region but how and when did it become a premium vineyard site? These days, when Napa and Sonoma wines are famous for their quality, it's easy to forget that for much of their history they grew inexpensive grapes. Truly little of their fruit was made into wine inside the counties.

Instead, starting in the 1800's, they were shipped to wineries closer to the city, and there was rarely a mention of a grape variety or location, the wines were red or white, sweet or hearty. Thanks to a number of cultural, economic and governmental reasons, the shift in the region from jug wines to premiums started in the 1970's. Then it really took off after the turn of the millennium.

While the location of a winery is flexible, the location of the vineyards is not.

From the cool southern edges of the bay to the warm tops of the valleys, the climate changes dramatically. This is due to the influence of the bay, the ocean and the rocky hills bordering the northern valleys, which are perfect for capturing the sun's heat. Napa is warmer than Sonoma because it's farther from the cool Pacific. Also, Napa Valley has Mount Saint Helena towering over its northern edge, *protecting it from the* north *winds.* Farming is all about location, so the growers carefully choose the best vineyard sites for the types of wine they want to make.

Traditionally, the growing areas like the Sonoma Valley and Napa's Oakville were always more popular because the warmth helps the grapes ripen sooner. In a competitive, bulk market, growers want their grapes to be ready to harvest as early as possible. *Only a certain number of grapes are going to be sold every year* and the sooner you can get to market the better chance you have of selling every bunch for the best price.

Also, the sooner you brought in the fruit, the less chance your crop would be damaged by any early rains. In the past when there were plenty of vineyard sites to go around, that left cooler Los Carneros and nearby Coombsville as suitable places to raise cattle, sheep and horses.

The rise of Los Carneros as a place to grow premium grapes is an interesting and complicated story. In the early days up-valley growers planted Riesling,

Pinot Noir and Chardonnay next to the Cabernet, Merlot and Zinfandel. But the regions where those diverse varieties thrive in Europe are hundreds and sometimes thousands of miles apart, with quite different climates. To understand why growers would move vineyards to a cooler climate we need to understand how vines work. The bright flavors that we so enjoy in wines are made in the grapes from sunlight and the deep flavors are contributed by the wood.

When Galileo said, *"Wine is water held together by sunshine,"* in many ways, he was correct. Imagine the sun rising in the vineyard, the earth warming and the sap creeping up the vine towards the grapes. As the sap moves through those twists and turns, it creates the aromatic textures that give the wine its foundation. That's why an older, kinkier vine produces more flavor than a young one with its smooth trunk. Vines need about one hundred days of the sap rising and falling to make enough of these complex, textured flavors to create an exceptional wine.

The red Burgundy grape Pinot Noir, thanks to its thin skin, will quickly produce enough alcohol for an entertaining wine. But, that hot, daylong sunshine found in the upper valleys helps the grapes produce sugar so quickly that the vine's sap doesn't have enough days to create those deeper flavors that give it character.

That's like a great looking person with *lots of sex appeal, but not a thought in their head!* They're attractive short-term, but iffy for a committed relationship. Who helped the local growers figure out where to plant their delicate, refined Pinot Noir vines, and their favorite companion grape, Chardonnay?

In the 1970s the godfather of winemaking in the North Bay was a diminutive Russian émigré named André Tchelistcheff. He came from a wealthy Russian family that had left the service of the Tzar during the revolution. After being *left for dead on the battlefield* in the conflict between the Red and White Russian armies, André arrived in Paris. There he studied winemaking, eventually arriving at the Pasteur Institute in Paris, which was the Mecca of the still new fermentation sciences.

Georges de La Tour, a Frenchman and chemist who was the head of Beaulieu Vineyards in Napa, found André there and invited him to be his winemaker. Since André had the required adventurous blood, he came to California and took the reins at Beaulieu and later Buena Vista. Thanks to his personal genius and the lack of restraints found in a new world winery, he proved to be an amazing innovator in wine technology.

Besides his career crafting some of America's early great wines, he was also the most important vineyard consultant in the region, responsible for planning numerous important winery properties. You can bet that if André once laid out the plans for their original vineyards, that factoid is going to appear on a winery's website. When you visit Beaulieu, there's a life-sized statue of André in the garden outside the reserve room.

In a funny twist of *hero worship*, when the Culinary Institute of America bought the Copia Center for Wine, Food and the Arts in downtown Napa, they commissioned a copy of the statue, but they enlarged it. They felt that a 'true to size' sculpture of the 4' 11" André was not impressive enough for the entranceway, so he got pumped up!

In the 1970s when the pace of grape growing accelerated and investments started flowing into the North Bay wineries, André, with Pinot Noir and Chardonnay cuttings in hand, led the charge to Los Carneros. He explained to everyone who would listen that it was *too hot up valley for these cool weather vines.* If they would plant the vines in the cooler climate that they preferred, they would make better wines. He was right!

It was around that time when promoters started calling Los Carneros the *'Burgundy of America,'* after France's primary Pinot producing region. It's the only AVA, or American Viticultural Area, which is shared by Napa and Sonoma. That's probably because it was established in the early 1980s before Napa was such a prominent brand.

They wouldn't share an AVA today because Napa *does not play well with others* and it's very protective of its brand name. Although, with Los Carneros, there's good justification for including the entire area as one district. Along the entire length it has a similar climate and geology, and a limited number of premium grape varieties grow well there.

Trying to grow warmer weather grapes like Cabernet or Merlot in Los Carneros often produces green pepper flavors that appear when the grapes struggle to ripen completely. From my own narrow perspective,

I wonder if the Sonoma Coast is a better example of the American Burgundy, with their great forests and ocean influence. The Pinot Noir from there shows that classic earthy depth of flavor more easily. In contrast, based on the spectacular Vermentino wines, an Italian white variety that I've had from Los Carneros, I wonder if calling it the 'American Cinque Terra' would be more accurate?

When the lines for the AVA were drawn, Napa made their part of Los Carneros larger than Sonoma's by generously extending it *up into the rolling hills* at the foot of Mount Veeder. In Sonoma they were more conservative with their pen. The Sonoma side of Los Carneros tightly hugs the bay and stops at the road that connects the two counties called predictably, Carneros Highway.

Just north of the road, the vineyards are considered to be in the Sonoma Valley AVA, even though that area south of the Sonoma Plaza grows the same grape varieties as Los Carneros. They felt that the Sonoma Valley AVA, which had been created a few years before, was a stronger brand than Los Carneros, but they didn't want to let Napa claim the AVA all for itself. *This tradition of drawing lines for the maximum financial advantage has a long tradition in California.*

In 1850 when it was about to become a state, California insisted on drawing its own borders. That's why the northeast border is on the far side of the gold-bearing mountains, to the detriment of Nevada. At the southern border, the line cants to the southwest to place the spectacular San Diego Harbor inside the United States, over the objections of Mexico.

I don't know if André had counted fully on the advantages that come from those dependable Carneros winds. Not only do they reduce the alcohol levels, but they help the grapes retain the valuable acids that clean the palate between bites, making the food taste better. It also helps your digestion by supplementing the stomach acid, which gets weaker as we get older. While a low acid wine like white Zinfandel is so soft on the palate that it makes a great cocktail drink, it doesn't make a meal taste better.

But a high-acid, Los Carneros wine excels at that. Also, the three acids in grapes contribute to the flavor and appeal, with tartaric being the savory acid most associated with wine. The citric acid that is common in oranges and lemons, and the malic acid that is found in apples contribute their own grace notes, although winemakers will often work to tone down the malic acid.

When wine is aged in oak barrels, a significant amount of that *malic acid is converted into lactic acid*, also found in fermented dairy. In red wines that softens the wine but in white wines it can also create the buttery flavor found in some popular chardonnays.

When grapes are grown in a location where it stays hot at night, the vines dump the acids, so the winemakers add tartaric acid because it's an essential part of wine's signature flavor! But those wines lack dimension, although they have plenty of alcohol. That's why those cold Los Carneros nights, which make the vines shiver, make all the difference when the wine gets to the glass. To give you an idea of how much winemakers value the acids in a grape, when the final product lacks that important structural feature they call it a 'flabby wine.' There's no situation when 'flabby' can pass as a compliment and you would never describe the cool climate Los Carneros wines that way!

Starting in the 1970s, as news of the area's potential spread, the European winemakers took notice. When they heard Chardonnay and Pinot Noir they thought Champagne, because those are the preferred grapes used in their famous sparkling wines. *As a result,* when you are standing at the foot of the Napa Valley on the patio at Domaine Carneros, owned by the Taittinger family from Champagne, France, European winemakers surround you. Across the road to the south, Cuvaison Estate Wines is owned by the Schmidheiny family from Switzerland. 'Cuvaison' in French is the process of extracting the colors and flavors from the skins of the grapes.

To the north, across the Carneros Highway and just beyond the di Rosa sculpture park, is the Artesa Winery, owned by Spain's oldest winemaking family, Raventós Codorníu. The name Artesa means *'craftsman'* in Catalan, the language in the region around Barcelona where the family is from. The modern, minimalistic building is tucked between two hills and built into the top of a third. They began by making sparkling wines in Napa in the early 1980's but ran into two roadblocks.

First, Americans *don't drink as much sparkling wine* as Europeans. Second, they were in direct competition with Domaine Carneros, that also makes sparkling wines. But Domaine is more visible and conveniently located in a grand Chateau that looks like a brick wedding cake, dramatically towering over the road. In comparison, Artesa is tucked in the hills, down a small road, in an earth covered building. It's a remarkable experience once you get inside, but you need to know that it's there! This must have been *very embarrassing* for the Codorníu family who have been making wine since the 1500s. How do they explain to the rest of the family that their winery in Napa is in the red? But, once they recognized the issues they shifted their focus to still wines, which Americans drink in abundance, and sales improved dramatically.

Just to the west of Artesa are the Carneros vineyards of Mumm (The French pronunciation is like moon, but with the M at the end /m/u:/m/ Moom), another French company from Champagne. They very smartly did not place their winery here. Instead, their winery and tasting room are halfway up the Napa Valley on the Silverado Trail in Rutherford. Because they are the only sparkling wine producer in the neighborhood, they have the dual advantage of being unique and convenient.

Further to the west, over the county line in Sonoma's Los Carneros, Gloria Ferrer from Spain produces marvelous sparkling wines on their large estate. They are *one of the first wineries you see* when you come north from San Francisco and their vineyards are spread out alongside the road at the foot of the hills. They chose that land because it reminded them of the area around their Catalan vineyards, so they built a rambling Spanish style winery. They dug caves for aging under the winery and built an exceedingly popular and expansive patio that looks over their vineyards to the northern edges of the bay. Obviously, the Europeans love Los Carneros and the fact that it's such a short drive from San Francisco ensures them plenty of visitors.

After an absence of many years, the herds of *grazing sheep have returned to Los Carneros*. Once the winter rains have filled the rows between the bare vines with tall grass and yellow mustard, you can see their fluffy white coats between the vines. Their gradual grazing works better than any plow at restoring the health of the land.

As they consume the springtime greens, they fertilize the land, while their hooves stomp on the bugs, promoting the secret life of the soil where flavor begins in magical ways. We are seeing them among the vines throughout the region, in part because a vineyard tended by sheep rather than rototillers eventually needs half as much water.

That quality is incredibly valuable in perpetually parched California. Whenever we see a flock of 'los carneros' grazing between the vines, we look for their *guardian dogs nearby,* keeping an eye open for coyotes and mountain lions, and looking right at home.

For all the large wineries in Los Carneros, there are still plenty of family ranches producing much smaller volumes of high-quality wine. Between the vineyards of Artesa and Mumm are the Fulton Vineyards, whose line of flagpoles, perched on a rise, can be seen from the Carneros Highway. It can be hard for a grape grower, living on their own land, dealing with the ramifications of decisions made in distant corporate boardrooms on the other side of the ocean.

Clearly, as a statement of their independence, the Hudson family runs the *'Jolly Roger' pirate flag* up their western-most flagpole twice a year. This is done to celebrate bud-break in the Spring when the vines first show their new leaves, and at harvest time, when the grapes are coming into the winery. This is a bay area custom that is popular among family businesses when they are surrounded by corporate entities. Flying the 'Jolly Roger' also brings a *smile* to those passing by.

Above: General Mariano Guadalupe Vallejo
Opposite: Sonoma Mission

Chapter Four
They All Came to Sonoma

One of California's most historic and charming locations, the Sonoma Plaza, is only half an hour's drive north of the Golden Gate. It's a spacious, tree-covered park with Mediterranean roots, which provides a central square for a town hall, stores, restaurants and cafes for the locals to meet. The only thing the Plaza lacks is an 'active church' although the historic Sonoma Mission's chapel on the northeast corner once filled that role. Surprisingly for such a tiny town, it's California's largest Plaza, so it easily accommodates the symmetrical city hall at its center.

The building was constructed with four identical sides to please the tax paying shopkeepers, because none of them wanted their stores to face the back of the building. Sonoma's special place in California history starts with being the northernmost, and final official outpost of the Spanish Empire in the Americas, and the final Franciscan Mission. I like to think that the explorers got this far and said, "Clearly we've arrived in Eden, this is far enough."

In front of the Sonoma Mission is a metal shepherd's crook with a bell at its top. These markers appear along the southern half of California on the historic path of El Camino Real. This "Royal Road" connected Spanish settlements together in North America.

In California most notably, it traveled between the twenty-one missions from San Diego to Sonoma where the Royal Road ended. Despite its grand title, in many places it would have been a narrow, horse trodden pathway, fringed with yellow mustard flowers.

The Plaza was laid out in 1835 by General Mariano Guadalupe Vallejo, a native born "Californio", who was the Spanish, and then Mexican commandant of Northern California. He hired a British sailor to help him survey the streets of the town. The old salt had good navigation skills because they aligned the streets quite accurately with the true compass directions.

The arrangement of the Plaza is *a bit unconventional.* Like most plazas it connects to four roads at the corners. But the Sonoma Plaza also had to accommodate El Camino Real, which connected to the center of the Plaza at the southern edge. Today it is called Broadway and when you drive up it towards the Plaza you are pointed due north! That same 'broad way' also once connected the Plaza to the docks twelve miles south on the San Pablo Bay. There the road heads west before turning south and following the edge of the bay to the Mission town of San Rafael.

The dramatic result of this design is that today, when visitors approach downtown Sonoma, they drive up a wide road lined with trees shading attractive homes, and arrive at the center of the Plaza, with the picturesque city hall directly in front of them.

The terrain between the Plaza and the bay is level, fertile farmland. So, when the General built a tower at the north edge of the Plaza, beside the barracks, any soldier on watch could see for many miles to the south. To the north, the land rapidly rises into a ridge of heavily forested hills that protect the town from the winter winds coming down the valley. *This was a wise choice for the town's location, and it was entirely thanks to General Vallejo.*

In contrast, the Franciscans had originally established the Mission in a less than ideal location six miles south, closer to the bay where it was subject to the relentless 'Carneros wind' and the nightly fogs!

Today the Cline Family Winery sits on that site. The family constructed a Mission Museum on their property, featuring models of the twenty-one missions built by German craftsmen for The Golden Gate International Exposition in 1939. The models had been in storage for many years when they were put up for auction and the Cline's purchased the entire lot, and then had them restored.

Northern California at that time was considered the 'ends of the earth,' where you sent your 'red headed stepchild' to make their fortune. If they did good, that's great, and if they didn't, well, who would know? Yet, the adventurous at heart from around the world kept finding their way there and as a result, seven different national flags have flown over Sonoma. You can see them in front of the city hall and around the corner at the Sebastiani Winery, next to the area's oldest vineyard site.

The flags start with England, when Sir Francis Drake planted his colors at Bodega Bay, during his circumnavigation of the globe in the 1600's in his ship, the Golden Hind. Then in 1820 Sonoma saw the flag of Imperial Spain raised with the establishment of the Presidio, or Fort, after which the Mission was relocated there.

Then the Spanish flag was replaced with that of Imperial Mexico under the Emperor Maximillian, a nephew of Napoleon. Next, power was wrested away from Maximillian in the Mexican Revolution, most flamboyantly by Pancho Villa. When the flag of the Republic of Mexico was raised the new government, in faraway Mexico City, secularized the missions, considering them, justifiably, as an instrument of the monarchy.

Someplace in this mix the flag of Imperial Russia flew at their Fort Ross, or 'Rossiya,' (Ruh-syee-yuh) for 'Mother Russia.' They established their 'fort' on the Northern Sonoma coast to grow food for their settlements in Alaska, under the noses of the Spanish and English, who had previous claims nearby. They also launched expeditions of Kodiak hunters from

Alaska along the California coast aboard American sailing ships, to hunt the sea otters for their precious pelts.

On June 14th, 1846, coincidentally America's 'Flag Day', American revolutionaries, mostly from Napa, raised the Bear Flag of the California Republic on the Plaza, in front of the barracks. Soon after, the first American naval ship of the line sailed into the San Francisco Bay, and the next flag to fly over Sonoma was the American. Sonoma became the United States military headquarters for Northern California and was frequented by numerous Civil War generals. *The old officer's quarters are still there* on Spain Street, walking distance from the Plaza, is the home of the commandant, Colonel Hooker, a Civil War hero. So, even though it was far from everywhere important at that time, plenty of countries wanted to stake a claim to Sonoma.

In the 1800's Sonoma was a mix of the native tribes, colonial Spanish, adventurous Americans, hospitable Russians and finally the industrious Chinese. The first Chinese ship sailed through the Golden Gate in 1850. In drawings and paintings of the wineries from that era, large numbers of Chinese workers are seen carrying and crushing grapes.

The oldest wine caves were dug by Chinese workers, who also cleared vineyards and built the bordering stone walls. From a Eurocentric point of view, it's important to realize that even though the Spanish left a cultural mark on colonial Sonoma, it sits on the Pacific Rim, where the Asian influence is ancient and pervasive. The one flag that has not been acknowledged is that of the

Chinese Admiral Zheng He, whose ships came to the California coast in the 1400s, as one of his seven Treasure fleets that sailed the globe and created the first known world maps.

The West Coast is littered with *artifacts left behind by the great treasure fleet;* stone anchors, buried shipwrecks and armor. The early Spanish cartographers frequently postulated locations for a Chinese city on the Northern California coast, that they named Quivira. That is also the name of a Northern Sonoma winery in the Dry Creek Valley, where the founder once displayed their collection of those historic maps in a small gallery beside the tasting room. Unfortunately, when they sold the winery, the maps left with them.

In the late 1800s, thirty percent of the Sonoma Plaza was filled with Chinese shops. At that time the important destination was a pair of towns several miles north of the Plaza thanks to numerous healing hot springs, around which hotels had sprung up to serve guests coming from the city.

After the 1906 earthquake that devastated San Francisco, the springs mysteriously receded into the earth and the businesses dried up. Today, only the Sonoma Mission Inn remains, and it accesses the deep mineral springs with a well. The rest of those investors moved south to the Plaza, forcing the Chinese businesses out.

In so many ways a plaza is different from a park, because it's a central meeting place for the community. Similar layouts are found in plazas throughout southern Europe and Northern Africa, remnants of the Roman

Empire which once ruled that part of the world. When Roman armies made camp, they used a similar layout, with a large open space for the troops to assemble, directly to the south of the commander's tent, or their house if it was a winter camp. General Vallejo, a classically trained soldier, mimicked that arrangement, and placed his initial home and headquarters on the northern edge of the Plaza, where he drilled his troops.

Despite the many purposes the Plaza has been used for over the years, today it is a beautiful location, thanks to the Women's Club of Sonoma. In the early 1900's the Plaza was a wreck, with numerous holes where mud for the adobe buildings had been excavated, and the debris from its short use as a railway terminal. The local club took the initiative and began a landscaping and tree planting campaign which yielded wonderful results.

Today there are two playgrounds, picnic tables, a duck pond, a band shell, a Visitors Center in an old Carnegie library, and plenty of space for multiple outdoor events like art and car shows. It is all wonderfully shaded by a spectacular and diverse grove of trees. There is also a charming statue of a seated General Vallejo, who would be pleased to see how the Plaza has evolved.

At the time when the Spanish established a Mission and Fort in San Francisco their resources were stretched *ridiculously thin*. They had colonies in south, Central and North America and bases in the far-off Philippines. The Missions depended on enslaving the local tribes people to operate, but there were very few trained soldiers available to enforce that. It was improbable that the Spanish could maintain control over California with the feisty Americans so nearby, by both sea and land.

Considering the potential of the San Francisco Bay, the Spanish Governor couldn't resist putting a Fort and Mission there. Unfortunately, the San Francisco Dolores Mission, was well named, because *'Dolores' translates as 'Sorrows'* and it was not a happy place; cold, foggy, plagued with malaria and hard to supply.

Admittedly the monks did choose *the warmest spot in that very cool peninsula for the mission,* and the park nearby is the spot where modern San Franciscans go when they are craving some sunshine. Despite that the monks and native helpers often sickened, so forty difficult years later they established a sanatorium eleven miles north of the Golden Gate at the warmer and dryer Mission at Saint Rafael. So now they had two missions, that due to climate and distance, were about as effective as two drunks helping each other walk down the street.

Up to this time two highly capable Franciscan Fathers, Junipero Serra and Fermín de Lasuén, had been directing the establishment of these settlements from the lovely Mission at Carmel. By the time San Rafael was established the Spanish grip on California was getting increasingly wobbly. Even though it's only one hundred and twenty miles from Carmel to San Francisco, due to the dangerous fog bound entrance to the bay, the marshes, and some very unfriendly tribes, it was a hard trip by land and sea. That made the two northernmost missions of San Francisco and San Rafael less than prime posts.

When a brash young Franciscan from Barcelona named Jose Altimira arrived in Carmel, Lasuén sent this unpleasant youngster to Mission Dolores, likely thinking, *"How much damage could he do?"*

Meanwhile to the north, the Russians had established their Fort Ross on the Sonoma Coast and were starting to trade further south. In this geopolitical game of chess, the Spanish commander wanted to establish a foothold in the North Bay to curtail that expansion. Since the Franciscan Missionaries worked hand in hand with the military, the young firebrand monk, Altimira, eventually proposed closing the missions in cool, wet San Francisco and nearby San Rafael, and using those resources to establish a mission farther north in Sonoma.

The commander gave him permission, and a few soldiers, to scout for a new site. This was a breach of protocol since he should have contacted the church fathers for permission, who, knowing Altimira, would have said no! But they set out to find a spot for the new spiritual outpost.

Of experience and judgment, Altimira was sorely lacking, because he chose a site in the first line of rolling hills above the bay. The location was cool, foggy, and perilously close to the malarial swamps that once lined the bay. It was barely an improvement on Yerba Buena, as San Francisco was known. At least on the bay they were close to the docks that brought their supplies. He called it the 'Mission San Francisco,' so now there were two of them. Why didn't he establish the settlement ten miles north in the warm, dry Sonoma Valley, a virtual paradise for growing food? Because they encountered native tribes that were not very welcoming to these interlopers. Even though he established the new mission, the Franciscans never closed the one in the south, so to differentiate between them they added the name Solano to the Sonoma Mission, for a south American missionary who had been made a Saint.

Altamira was remarkably bad at endearing himself to the native people, whom they depended upon for converts and labor. To save him from harm the Franciscan Fathers in Carmel quickly transferred him to another mission. Soon after the government in Mexico decreed that all Spanish born people, unwilling to become Mexican citizens, must leave Alta California and he returned to Spain, never to be heard from again, although his name graces a Sonoma Middle School.

A while later, now 'General' Vallejo, who had a keen eye for real estate, moved the mission to the warmth and safety of the Sonoma Plaza, where it sits today as a state museum. So that is how downtown Sonoma ended up in the only nearby valley without a river.

Today the population of the little City of Sonoma is just over 10,000 people. Considering the expansiveness of the Plaza, I suspect that the General expected it to grow much larger with time. But despite being at the base of a wonderfully fertile valley, as an economic center, it suffered from a serious flaw. There is no river or docks, and without those there would be no boats nearby to economically carry the farm produce to market. Most major cities are on navigable rivers. The exceptions are places like Denver, which is a stopping off point before crossing the mountains. Even though Rome's Tiber River only handles small boats, it became a commercial center because travelers on the ancient salt trail could safely ford the river there.

The Spanish choice of Sonoma as a Pueblo, or official city, and a military base seems odd, because just to the west is the city of Petaluma, which sits on the northern edge of the navigable Petaluma River. About the same distance to the east is the city of Napa, on the banks of the navigable Napa River. Maybe General Vallejo thought Petaluma too cold and Napa too hot, so Sonoma in the middle was just right, and at the center of the territory he firmly controlled.

There was one *unexpected benefit that came from Sonoma being an economic backwater,* compared to its neighboring cities with their navigable rivers; it remained small and frugal. So, rather than replacing older buildings with newer construction, including the original and very charming adobes, they could only afford to repair what they had.

As a result, downtown Sonoma has a wonderful collection of buildings from the founding period of California. In comparison, larger and wealthier Napa and Petaluma have an impressive collection of European style stone buildings that were constructed later in the 1800's and early 1900's, when lumber and wine shipping created a steady stream of wealth.

As roads and cars improved, the quaint nature of Sonoma, with its history, wine and charming Plaza, became wonderfully attractive to tourists wanting to spend a day in the country. The tiny town of Sonoma is the most historic spot in California, a commonwealth that, in land mass, is similar to Japan or Italy.

Here's why! Sonoma was home to California's 21st and final Franciscan mission. It was also the sixth and final official Spanish city, or 'Pueblo'. Then it was one of a handful of official forts, or Presidios. It is the only town in California that has all three of these historical distinctions. Finally, it's the 'Philadelphia of California,' because the Sonoma Plaza was where California declared itself the Independent Republic of California. They raised the 'Bear Flag' there on the northeastern corner of the Plaza in front of the Mexican soldier's barracks, which are still there today as part of the state park.

You can recognize the site by the statue celebrating the 'Bear Flaggers.' Their choice of the 'Bear' flag, which is today the state flag, is due to an interesting piece of history. At the time the settlers arrived, the North Bay had one of the largest populations of California grizzly bears on the West Coast. To stay safe the early settlers were forced to make their homes up in the trees, and for tribes outside the region the word 'Napa' meant grizzly bear.

While all this sounds quite heroic, there's some shading that we need to add to the story. The Bear Flaggers who bearded General Vallejo in his den included about thirty Americans, mostly from Napa. They had heard rumors that the Mexican government was going to force them out. While this was proposed by the Governor in Monterey, it was not very likely. First of all, there were lots of Americans in the area, mostly arriving by ship, although some came over the mountains via the Donner Pass. Second, General Vallejo liked the Americans, he gave many of them land for services rendered, and he was having a hard enough time finding Mexicans and Native People to develop the wonderful farm and grazing land.

So, he wasn't inclined to force out any good prospects. He told people that his birthday was on July fourth, Independence Day, even though it was actually on the fifth, because he felt that California's future was with the United States. Also, he depended on the American sailing ships to bring him needed goods.

In fact, his house was brought from *New England* in pieces in the belly of *an American sailing ship*. Later he bought a second house, transported the same way, that he gave to his daughter. Both houses stand today, one on a local park made from the Vallejo Farmstead, and the other as a restaurant on Spain Street called predictably, 'The General's Daughter.'

Was it good luck or planning, that the revolutionaries arrived at the barracks when the General's soldiers were away on missions? General Vallejo was there by himself, with an armed company of former soldiers on his front steps. So, he invited the leaders in to talk and broke out the brandy, of which he was one of the North Bay's biggest producers.

The discussion was long-winded, because after the leaders had not emerged for several hours, they sent another representative inside, who found the little group having a wonderful time. But rather than returning to make a report to the waiting band, they also joined in the festivities. Eventually the General invited everyone to his place for dinner and the first day of the revolution came to an inebriated close.

That custom of the Plaza being a place for hospitality, and the coming together of people to find a common ground is a long tradition that continues there today.

The final Shepherd's Crook and Bell at the Sonoma Mission Marking the Route of the Camino Royale

Chapter Five
The Magical Valley of the Moon

As you travel north from San Francisco through the hills of Marin County, when you turn east at the top of the bay you quickly enter the lower edges of Sonoma County. As you go over a low hill called Sears Point, that can be seen from miles away on the bay, you are in the Los Carneros region, known for its windy, cool climate and extensive chardonnay and pinot noir vineyards. As you travel north you enter the lovely Sonoma Valley. The rocky Mayacamas Mountains form the valley's eastern side while the graceful Petaluma Hills and Sonoma Mountain form the western edge. Twelve miles north of the bay you come to the little, charming town of Sonoma.

The origin of the name Sonoma has invited many opinions. In the native Patwin or Pomo languages Sonoma means the Valley of the Moon. So, the name, Sonoma Valley, means 'Valley of the Moon' Valley! Odd, but in California there are many examples of names made up of merged languages. *The North Bay has more native names than much of California* because the local tribes were prosperous, the grizzly bears were fierce, and the three competing groups of colonizers were stretched thin as they vied for control. Sonoma is a popular name used in numerous brands, Williams Sonoma being the most famous, having started his store steps from the Plaza.

Locally it seems like every other organization and business is called 'Sonoma' something or other, including the County of Sonoma, the City of Sonoma, the Sonoma Plaza, the Sonoma Valley, Sonoma Mountain, the Sonoma Women's Club and half of the businesses.

Surprisingly, there's no Sonoma River and that is a place where the historic city was short-changed, because Napa to the east and Petaluma to the west both have navigable rivers, not surprisingly named for them. From their downtown docks you can sail to the bay, the Pacific Ocean and the world beyond.

But Sonoma Valley is drained by a humble, but pretty stream called predictably, Sonoma Creek. The northern part of the county is drained by the long, but shallow Russian River, which empties into the Pacific north of Bodega Bay. But the only craft traveling along that waterway, as it wends its way through vineyards and forests are canoes, rafts and inner tubes filled with vacationers.

The complete story of the name 'Sonoma' is complicated by the remarkable history of the North Bay, which I've been told is the longest continuously occupied region in North America. For people who understand agriculture that fact is not surprising, because the geology and climate are especially favorable for humans and the plants that feed them. A good part of California has the prized Mediterranean climate, and the North Bay is the center of that zone. It's a place of warm, dry days with brilliant sunshine, and cool, humid nights.

We owe credit for the translation of the name Sonoma to a giant of the literary world, Jack London. He was a hard living, hard drinking, cigarette smoking adventurer. As a teenager he'd been an 'oyster pirate' on the San Francisco Bay, in a boat that he bought with money borrowed from the part-African American, part-Caucasian woman who raised him. When he returned from prospecting in Alaska with empty pockets, he became America's most successful author by writing about his time there.

Later, Jack taught himself how to navigate by the stars while sailing to Hawaii. As money rolled in, he bought a thousand acres on the slopes of Sonoma Mountain, above the tiny town of Glen Ellen, that he called his "Beauty Ranch." He practiced an early version of sustainable agriculture and railed at his neighbors for their less environmentally friendly practices. While he grew wine grapes on vineyards that are still there, he didn't make wine. So, he would ride his horse down the hill to his neighbors who were very proper, church-going folks, whose busy farm included a sawmill, vineyards and most importantly, a winery. He would hitch his horse to a rail outside their office and purchase some bottles. The Missus disliked the colorful Mr. London's lifestyle and the moment he was late in his accounts, she would cut him off.

Some of her resentment may have come from the strained arrangement of their property lines, often an issue in farming communities, because Jack's ranch surrounded their lovely little valley. Their land had been a grant from General Vallejo, in thanks for carpentry work that the husband had done repairing Sonoma's Mission building. Today that ranch is the site of the Benziger Family Winery, with its elegant, terraced vineyards. The original farm buildings where Jack used to hitch his horse on his wine runs are still there, although under occasional attack by some particularly aggressive woodpeckers.

At the time when Jack London settled in Sonoma, there were several native tribes in the area that had been converted to Christianity by the Franciscan Missionaries and allied themselves with General Vallejo. Most notable among them was Sem-Yeto, who everybody called Chief Solano. At six foot, seven inches tall he was an impressively powerful man. He took his name from the San Francisco Solano Mission in Sonoma where he was educated, after being kidnapped as a child from the Suisun tribe over the mountains to the east.

Sem-Yeto was a close friend of the General and quite a famous personality in the region and seen as the titular head of all the Sonoma tribes. *The Chief took quite a fancy to the Russian Princess Helene de Gagarin,* the wife of General (or Count depending on the telling) Alexander Rotscheff from Fort Ross. Sem-Yeto made plans to kidnap her with the help of the other chiefs. But Vallejo talked him out of that, by describing how the combined forces of the Spanish and the Russians would set out to annihilate the tribes. So, for the sake of his people he sacrificed his desire for the blonde beauty.

It's funny that the two Missions named for Saint Francis are at the far northern edge of his order's circle of influence in the Americas. Supposedly, as Friar Junipero Serra sailed up the California coast naming bays for every saint except their patron, he told the soldiers that Francis would let him know when they had come to his place.

Since the San Francisco Bay is among the world's greatest, it seemed a natural fit. It was only through a later misguided effort to move the Mission to Sonoma, that they ended up with two missions named for Francis, which the Franciscans seemed fine with. What's interesting is that the Sonoma Mission, which takes its primary name from the native language, is the only one that has a memorial to the many native people who lived and served there.

When Jack London settled into his new home in the early 1900's there was still a large population of native people in the area. It's not surprising that Jack London, who made his living as a writer, asked around about the meaning of Sonoma. A local Chief told him that Sonoma meant the *Valley of the Seven Moons*. That makes sense since the Patwin word for Moon is 'Sanar,' from which Sonoma is a short trip, especially if the word for place, or home is 'Ma.' That is coincidentally one of the first 'words' that babies make, hence: mom, mama, madre, mother. Also, the Sonoma Valley where Jack lived is crescent, or Moon shaped so it all fits.

When trying to understand why they would say seven moons we need to realize that, unlike today, the native people would have had a more personal relationship with the sky. The Sun ruled their days, and the Moon their nights. Nighttime travel was timed to the lunations. Venus was the most beautiful jewel in their sky while Mars looked blood red. Mercury shone brightly for the briefest moments like the arrival of a brilliant idea. Jupiter and Saturn's orbits marked the longer cycles of life. Maybe seven Moons was a mistranslation for the Pomo word for *the seven celestial bodies,* the Sun, Moon and Planets, that all of humanity has watched travel through the heavens during countless millennia.

But they were not the only pre-Columbian residents of Sonoma with sky knowledge. We know that Chinese sailors were left behind by the Treasure fleets in the 1400's. Besides the stone anchors and armor later discovered, the Bay Area also has a very long wall in the east bay. It was built with the same construction techniques used in China's Great Wall, and its origin has never been explained. The Spanish encountered tribes in Northern California that wore Chinese style clothes and hair styles. In the late 1800's a state anthropologist found a tribe of 'Indians' living in the Russian River Valley's redwood forests *that only spoke Chinese.*

Sailors, more than most people, are tied to the stars. Traveling the open seas, devoid of distracting light under the dome of the heavens, they depend on the seven celestial bodies that travel the ecliptic for guidance. The Chinese were among the ancient world's most advanced astronomers and cartographers, and their *Astrologers* considered the planets reflections of the social hierarchy on Earth. The Sun was the Emperor, the Moon the Empress, Mercury their secretary, messenger and servant, Venus represented the court ladies, while Mars represented the court guards, Jupiter stood for the educated Mandarins and Saturn stood for the Priests.

They observed the planets as they changed positions, and angled for power, meeting, separating, and shaping the fates of those below. *The Chinese Compass, or Bagua, is used for both navigation and Feng Shui.* It divides the world into eight directions, seven for the celestial bodies, and one for the Earth beneath our feet. How much of the Chinese sailor's knowledge seeped into the lore of the native tribes?

Compared to sunnier, warmer Napa, Sonoma has always been considered mysterious. It is divided into numerous unique valleys, towering redwood forests and convoluted coastlines. The climate and geology vary widely, but among all these diverse locations Sonoma Valley is special. It was formed in a gentle crescent between two lines of mountains, the remains of ancient volcanoes and uplifted seabed, that are steep, but not inaccessible. It is only fifteen miles long and varies between one and two miles wide. At its northern edge is the broad Santa Rosa plain. To the south are gently rolling hills that turn into the marshes of the San Pablo Bay.

The little City of Sonoma sits like a pearl in the lower third of its elongated crescent. The valley sits in a magic zone, where everything grows well. There are numerous underground springs that not only provide the plants with water, but also minerals. The soil is especially good at *holding onto that water,* and because the valley is narrow it loses less moisture to the hot sun. The valley angles from the northwest to the southeast, perfectly aligned with the warm, color rich mid-morning sunshine.

So, what is the source of the name Sonoma? There are so many possibilities. Who knows what the Chief was trying to explain when he 'translated' the name Sonoma? Who knows what Jack London actually heard? He was a great author whose mother was a mystic and Astrologer. In the starry arts the Moon symbolizes the mother, and the Valley of the Moon was where Jack made his *final home*. We're just lucky that he probably used some well-worn creative license to give us such a lovely name for this beautiful place.

Chapter Six
The Imperial Russian River Story

Names are different from other words in the way that we accept them. We think of words as part of a sentence communicating an idea, like interdependent planets in their own Solar System, spinning around the Sunny subject and Lunar object. But names are like comets and islands, sovereign nations accepted at face value, with all their complicated history.

Consider the name *Chardonnay*, a popular white wine grape that appears on many menus and wine lists. People rarely wonder about that name's origin or meaning. They assume it's French, since the most famous representatives are from Burgundy and Champagne. Most people think the name means something in a local Patois and thus, like so much about the French countryside, its history is obscure and complicated, like *Merlot*, which means *blackbird*. But Chardonnay's name instead traces back to the Middle East, Syria, Lebanon and Israel where the grape was found by the Crusaders. In those languages the name Chardonnay means the *Gates of God*, which says much about the importance they ascribed to that pretty, luminous grape and its tremendously adaptable wine.

Coincidentally, Chardonnay is one of the two most popular grapes grown in the North Bay region whose names also have complicated and exotic histories. One of those is the *Russian River Valley*. People rarely ask us about the source of that name, yet we've lost count of the number of clients who were surprised that the Russians settled that green expanse north of San Francisco. Why else would they call that shallow, winding river that carries the silt and scent of the mountains all the way to the Pacific, the 'Russian' River? People just accept names without thinking, like New Yorkers accept the Russian Tearoom, formed by members of the Imperial Ballet, and the Russian Baths, started by a German physician in the 1800's, even though both Manhattan icons are far from Saint Petersburg.

Why would the Russians come to Northern California? Well, why wouldn't they? Russia's eastern coast is opposite Sonoma's, and the Russians are good at navigating ice, whether it's on the Baltic Sea, or the Pacific port of Vladivostok. That seaside city sits at the tip of the broad Siberian plateau, a place that Americans view as a great wasteland, but it's an area of huge resources.

Whenever there are things to sell and deep-water ports welcoming ships, there's commerce and Vladivostok is Russia's gateway to the Pacific rim and America's west coast.

It's easy to forget now that *Russia once controlled Alaska,* which it sold to the United States in 1867 for two cents an acre. At the time it was called Seward's Folly, for the Secretary of State who negotiated the sale. Considering the gold and oil Alaska contains, that turned out to be a good deal. For the Russians, exploiting Alaska was difficult because of the great distances and harsh weather. While the fur trade was very profitable, sustaining the colony was a Labor of Hercules, because transporting food from Western Russia to Alaska over the Trans-Siberian Railway was an *exercise in futility.*

If the food wasn't stolen by officials or brigands along the way, it rotted during the long rail trip and ensuing sea voyage. To feed their people it was decided to look in a different direction. The most practical was to the south along the Pacific coastline where there was warmer weather, so two ships were dispatched to find a suitable location for their settlement.

As the Russians sailed south, they knew that the land where they were planning to settle, had been claimed for England in the late 1600s by Sir Walter Raleigh when he was circumnavigating the globe in his ship, the Golden Hind. But Sir Walter did not hang around to protect his claim, poor guy.

While he did return to England to acclaim, with a ship full of treasure, he missed discovering the inlet to the San Francisco Bay by about ten miles. This is considered one of the world's greatest harbors, protected from the weather and fed by an extensive, navigable river system. This is exactly what sailors searched the globe for. Unfortunately for him, the inlet is hard to find from the ocean side. Sir Walter was so close, but no cigar!

Instead, they landed just north of the inlet on the marshy shores of Point Reyes. Then they passed by the outlet of the Russian River, but found it *too shallow* and filled with sand bars to navigate with a sailing ship. Finally, the Golden Hind moored in little Bodega Bay before setting out across the deep blue waters of the Pacific to the spice islands.

The Russians also knew that the Spanish had claimed parts of California as far north as San Francisco. This was the northern tip of their overextended empire before they ventured into Sonoma. The Spanish military was sorely lacking in the neighborhood, so it was difficult for them to protect their claim, but that doesn't mean a little diplomacy wasn't in order.

The Russian Governor met with the Spanish Commandant in Monterey to get his 'permission' for the settlement. It didn't hurt that the dashing Governor *fell in love* with the Commandant's beautiful daughter, but that's another, very romantic but dramatically sad story.

In 1812 the Russians tactfully found a spot along the California Coast in Sonoma, seventy miles north of the Spanish settlements in San Francisco. They held onto it for the next thirty years developing farms, orchards and ranches. Surely it was a pleasant change from the frozen north and their seal hunting camps in Alaska.

It didn't take long for them to realize how well they had chosen. While there's plenty of sunshine along the coast during the day, the nightly fog keeps the hillsides green for much of the year, making it an ideal place for raising food and grazing their livestock. While much of this region is prone to drought, that coastal band can get up to fifty inches of rain yearly.

Sonoma, with its many diverse climates, is such a 'Garden of Eden' that the famous botanist, Luther Burbank, who developed many of our popular fruit varieties, said that *of all the places on Earth he had visited, this was the 'most blessed by nature.'* Everything grows well there, whether it's native or not, from palm trees to apples, from grapes to redwoods. Burbank bought his farm in Santa Rosa in 1875 and built greenhouses where he did his research. Admittedly, it was about forty miles east of the Russia camp on the softly rolling hills and plains between the warmer Sonoma Valley and the cooler Russian River Valley.

The Russians built a fort with four strong walls and cannons, but they didn't have any soldiers, only traders, trappers and administrators. After discovering how difficult it was to hunt the sea otters that live along the California coast, they brought Aleut hunters, and their women, south from Kodiak Island in Alaska. The otter's coats are extremely dense and soft, and *there was a lucrative market for them among the Chinese royalty.*

While the hunters, with their kayaks, traveled along the coast in American sailing ships, the women farmed the land, producing the vegetables and fruits that were shipped up north. *It was a strange place and the Aleut women claimed that little 'people', the Irish would call them Leprechauns, would come out at night, running around the camp and causing mischief,* It was a pretty wild place during the day too.

Apparently, among the traders and trappers, a favorite diversion was getting drunk and firing the cannons. It happened so often that the settlement's bookkeeper complained about the expense for gun power. Today, when you go on the historic tour, one of the highlights is the firing of the cannon. We highly recommend a visit!

Where did the name Fort Ross come from? Who was this guy named Ross? There was no such person! In fact, *this is an example of 'California-ese,' a dialect similar to 'Spanglish,'* where words from different languages are married together. The English word 'Fort' is married to 'Ross,' which comes from the Russian word 'Rossiya,' which means 'Mother Russia.' The 'Russians,' actually included a wide variety of Eastern Europeans.

A wonderful example are the Bohemian brothers, from what is today modern Poland, who established the Korbel Winery on the cool Western edge of the Russian River Valley in the mid 1800's. Their historic winery buildings, situated just north of the river, are surrounded by their vineyards and coastal redwood forests.

The local tribes liked the Russians because they were honest in their trading and easy to work with. They were much preferred to the imperious and crafty Spanish, who sought to convert the local tribes to Christianity using the harshest methods possible, including kidnapping and virtual slavery. In a land where most of the westerners were a pretty wild group, the 'Russians' were culturally a pleasant contribution.

They were led by the handsome and talented Count Alexander Rotscheff, and his *beautiful*, highly refined wife, the Princess Ilona de Gagarin. They lived there with their three children and a surprising number of comforts, including musical instruments, but that's admittedly, another long story!

Russia held onto their Fort until it became clear that California was going to become part of the United States, at which point they sold it to John Sutter, of later gold rush fame. Why did they give up such a prime location? There were geopolitical reasons behind that choice! Their involvement in the Crimean War was causing them to withdraw resources from the Pacific, and they hoped that America controlling the area would suppress the British naval presence in the region. Britain was their main adversary.

Remember, the Russians sold Alaska to the United States, a deal for which Secretary of State Seward was roundly criticized. Who knew that thirty-one years later gold would be discovered there, starting the massive gold rush. Not only did it dramatically increase Alaska's population, but it made fortunes for the west coast shipping companies that connected the mines to San Francisco. While this is all very interesting, I heard the inside story from a wine tour client who was an American history professor teaching in Russia. Apparently, the Russians gave up their holdings in Alaska and California because they were afraid that their people would become infected with American Democracy!

Even though the Russians gave up their 'fort', there are many Bay Area families that trace their roots back to that settlement on the Sonoma Coast, where their ancestors just wanted a warm place to raise their food and children. Russian Hill in San Francisco takes its name from an old graveyard for those fur trappers. Later, when the Russian Revolution deposed the Czar, many of the aristocracy fled to the United States via the Pacific Port of Vladivostok.

When they arrived in San Francisco, they settled on *Russian Hill*. Early on, when I was researching this book, I was befriended by a tour guide who was raised in San Francisco, and he filled me in on much of the local color. He was a *direct descendant* of the Russian Governor of Alaska and proof that the heritage of 'Fort Rossiya' lives on in the Bay Area.

Opposite: Ferrari-Carano Vineyards

Chapter Seven
Wine Country's Great Buildings

Wine Country has a wonderful collection of winery buildings. The first were built in the early 1800s, and many of those are still in use today. The builders began by using redwood, either found on the site, or brought from the towering forests that blanket the Pacific Coast. Even though those beautiful, red boards stand up well to bugs and rot, they are not as durable as stone. So, in the late 1800's the builders turned to masonry, which has long been considered the ideal material for a winery.

Stone is perfect for a building which needs to stay cool and humid while standing up to water and the acids found in wine. Starting in the 1970's there was an influx of international companies building dramatic wineries where the architecture would add to the attraction.

But when the Spanish first arrived in the North Bay, they just needed to make wine.

The region's first prominent winemaker was a native '*Californio*' and Spanish officer, General Mariano Guadalupe Vallejo, born in Monterey on July 4th, a date of which he was particularly proud due its affinity with the United States. Mariano produced wine under his label, 'Lachryma Montis,' or '*the Tears of the Mountain,*' named for the spring above his home in Sonoma. It was from his vineyards that *George Yount, mountain man and wagon train leader,* purchased the first grape vines planted in the heart of the Napa Valley. Yount's Caymus Spring Ranch was a grant from the General.

Those early winemakers planted high sugar Mission grapes and fermented them in tanks made from cow hides hung on a frame. But they soon learned from the winemakers who came there from Hungary, Prussia, France and Italy, who were well aware of the advantages that wooden tanks and stone buildings provided to the winemaker. The General's most obvious contributions to the local architecture are the historic buildings around the Plaza, and two notable houses, built in New England and transported by sailing ship to Sonoma, one for his home and another for his daughter.

The development of a winemaking region happens in stages, often over many generations. But Napa and Sonoma gained a great head start in the 1800s, thanks to a stream of cheap labor from Italy and China arriving through the Golden Gate. Italy's winemaking tradition predates the Romans, and in the 1800's it was their dominant industry. But the combination of diseased vines and drought sent thousands of young Italian men streaming to America in search of related work. In San Francisco, Chinese labor contractors would provide as many workers as a vineyard owner could afford. They did the backbreaking work of clearing the land and stacking the stones into long border walls that you can still see today.

They also dug the earliest *wine caves*. Later they built the dikes and levees that allowed thousands of acres of land along the edges of the bay to be reclaimed for farming, coincidentally eliminating the malarial marshes that once covered a third of the bay. The lines of fragrant *eucalyptus trees* that you see by the bay were part of that strategy. They pull a great deal of water out of the ground and the scent discourages the mosquitos. You still find old ranch houses in Los Carneros surrounded by orderly groves of tall, graceful eucalyptus.

Buena Vista Winery

Count Agoston Haraszthy built two of California's first stone winery buildings at Buena Vista in Sonoma in 1857. He was a great believer in the Chinese workers who cleared his vineyards and dug his caves. The 'Colonel,' as he was respectfully known locally, was a contemporary and friend of General Vallejo, to whom he was eventually related through the marriage of their children. Two of the Count's sons married two of the General's daughters. Haraszthy's two winery buildings are still in use today, which is a story in itself.

The buildings were damaged by a series of earthquakes, but the smaller of the two, used for brandy making, was repaired with *earthquake stars*. Those are the threaded endcaps that appear on the outside of the building when a steel rod has been installed to prevent the walls from spreading.

Often with these old buildings in an earthquake prone area, a veritable constellation will dot the outside. Today the brandy building serves as the tasting room, with a small museum upstairs. The larger of the two was the main winemaking building, but the damage it sustained was more challenging to repair, so it sat *unused* for many years while the winery went through several owners.

Finally in 2011 the new owner, Jean-Charles Boisset, began an extensive restoration. When the work was finished, wine was once again being produced in the grand building, more than 160 years after the first stones were laid. The remainder of the three-story building is devoted to hospitality spaces, including a wine tool museum and, of course, offices! The most remarkable part of that story was the way it was restored. Instead of depending on 'earthquake stars,' an expedient, yet sometimes ugly solution, they took a more expensive and demanding approach.

They removed the roof and drilled holes through the entire height of the stone walls and into the foundation. Then they placed *steel rods* inside the holes and filled them with epoxy, creating a new superstructure inside the walls. Today, visitors enjoy the winery that looks very much like it did when the Count was still walking on these grounds, talking about making his great wines in California.

As compared to Napa where there are more 'destination' wineries, Sonoma's tradition is bucolic and homey. One of its iconic houses from the 1920's is the white mansion on the Chateau Saint Jean property. Today it is used for winery hospitality, but it started as a home for a wealthy Midwestern family. By today's standards it is not big, but it is gracious and beautifully appointed, paneled with exotic woods and designed to take advantage of the views.

The family and the great botanist Luther Burbank were friends, and the beautiful gardens continue to reflect a love of gardening. It faces east and spreads out in a long line from north to south. On the west side, the two wings extend out to form a protected courtyard, perfect for watching the setting sun. On the southside *there once was a pond shaped* like the Great Lakes to remind them of their home in the Midwest.

Jordan Vineyard & Winery

In Northern Sonoma's Alexander Valley you will find the Jordan Winery, completed in 1979. It is a grand *chateau* in the French style, that stretches along the top of a hill, at the end of a long, curving drive. On one end are the offices. In the middle is the dramatic winery with its tall wooden tanks that had to be lowered into place before the roof was installed. At the other end are luxurious apartments for the wine club members. They face a spacious, hedge trimmed patio to relax on, with a glass of wine while you enjoy the view of the vineyard cascading down the slopes.

At the top of Northern Sonoma's Dry Creek Valley sits the very elaborate Ferrari-Carano Winery, with its beautiful gardens. This was built by the Carano family, starting in the early 1980's. They own casinos in Reno Nevada, and there may be a touch of that in its flamboyant style, because most of Northern Sonoma is pretty 'country'. The property has a *dual personality* because the two main buildings, one for winemaking and the other for hospitality, were built in two quite different styles. Aesthetically this seems odd to someone accustomed to the homogeneous nature of European wineries.

In Bordeaux, the great chateaus all share a similar look. In Italy, the grand villas follow traditional lines. But the long, rambling winery building at Ferrari-Carano is distinctly Japanese, which is funny since that country's winemaking tradition for centuries was primarily Saki.

When the Carano family built their impressive hospitality center in an elaborate Italianate manner and placed it on a scenic rise, opposite the winery. When you emerge from behind the hedge that separates the property from the parking lot, you see the elaborate, Italian style building on a rise at the end of a long walkway, bordered by a picture-perfect lawn. The building is not parallel to the walkway, or the winery, but canted inward so as you approach you can clearly see the front at an attractive angle.

Along the right side of the lawn is a high wall concealing a beautiful ornamental garden that incorporates both Asian and western motifs. You enter the garden just steps from the parking lot and emerge, thoroughly charmed by Mrs. Carano magical garden right before the building, bypassing the pathway.

Napa Makes a Change in the 1800's

Fortunately for the Napa winemakers, when they wanted to build their wineries in the late 1800's, Sonoma was awash in Italian immigrants, a culture with an ancient masonry tradition. Because Sonoma is so similar to Piedmont, Italy, boatloads of young Italian men came there looking for work. At that time the cheapest berth on a steamer was equivalent to a long-distance bus ticket today. Italy is a mountainous country blessed with abundant quarries of marble, granite, and alabaster, so the profession of mason is more common than that of carpenter. In Italy a wood parquet floor is considered a greater luxury than the more common marble.

Wine Country was not the only beneficiary of this migratory event. The wonderful stone buildings that grace our *Ivy League Universities* were built by Italian masons, whose descendants often still live in those towns. Most of America's stone churches and the most ornate of Washington DC's government buildings owe their stately beauty to those anonymous Italian stone masons and sculptors.

No matter how much an architect tries to impose their design style on a building, the people who use their hands to build it always get a vote. In downtown Napa the Italian craftsmen's influence on a very non-Italian building, is there for everyone to see. The historic Presbyterian Church on Third and Randolph was built in 1889. Traditionally, American Presbyterian churches are simpler than the elaborate Catholic Churches.

Yet this towering wooden building is dramatic, with its big stained-glass windows, and most notably, numerous figures adorning the outside, very much in the Roman Catholic style. Why? Because Italian craftsmen built it, and in their eyes, a church *needed statues of the Saints* adorning the exterior to welcome the congregation. More than likely the supervising architect was busy with another project, and by the time he came back the workers were putting away their tools and heading to another job site. Any changes cost extra!

Successful buildings need to stand up to the prevailing weather, even in California's lovely Mediterranean climate that is so kind to humans, grapes and olives. Visitors from colder climes are often surprised to hear that the mountaintops lining the valleys get traces of snow every few winters, like *the dusting of sugar* on top of an almond croissant from our famous bakeries. The Northern Italian masons seemed to have missed that point because they built substantial structures prepared to endure hundreds of years of rain, ice and snow, even though we don't do that kind of weather here!

That does explain why these great stone structures still look so good after twelve decades, despite having endured multiple earthquakes and thirty to forty years of abandonment due to Prohibition. Admittedly the mason's propensity to overbuild was thoroughly supported by the Vermont born, and New England trained architect and winery engineer Hamden McIntyre. He had built wineries in the Finger Lakes region of New York State and worked as a marine engineer in Canada and

Alaska. When the first stone wineries were being imagined McIntyre was working in San Francisco. He had come to California to help re-organize a newly formed shipping partnership, Hansen, Nybom and Company.

The youngest partner, whom *Hamden* befriended, was *Captain Gustave Niebaum,* a Finnish American ship captain who made a fortune shipping furs from Alaska. Gustave eventually changed the Finnish spelling of his name Nybom, to the German spelling in deference to his German Jewish partners.

As Niebaum grew increasingly wealthy, he dreamed of outfitting a ship and sailing the world with his beloved German American wife, and then buying a French Chateau. But Suzanne, born in California, didn't like boats, hated the ocean and didn't want to live in France, so far from her home. Instead, they decided to build Napa's first grand winery, naming it Inglenook, which they call a small, cozy seating nook, big enough for two, alongside a fireplace.

They built a Victorian mansion at the foot of the Mayacamas mountains in Rutherford, *with a carriage house where the captain made his first wine.* Gustave traveled throughout Europe as far east as Hungry, to observe wine making techniques. He brought back a wide variety of grape vines he planted in their vineyards, including many that are popular today. While Gustave and Suzanne Niebaum never had children, they adopted his wife's niece and nephew and raised them as their own.

In an interesting case of history repeating itself, many years later when the Coppola's bought the house.

Francis made his first wine in that same carriage house and called it Rubicon. As you might recall from Roman history, the Rubicon River was the northern border between Gaul and Italy. When Julius Caesar came back from his triumphant five years in what is today's modern France, his enemies in the Senate planned to ruin him in the courts. To save his honor he led a small portion of his army across the river, the official border of Italy, which made him a rebel. His famous quote as they road into the water was, *"Let the dice fly high."*

His enemies were so terrified by his approach that they abandoned the city, and the treasury stuffed with gold and he because the virtual ruler of Rome. By naming the wine Rubicon, they were saying that now that they made their first wine, there was no turning back.

But back to Niebaum's marvelous building. The captain wanted to build a state-of-the-art winery in Napa, thousands of miles from France so he engaged an architect who understood the aesthetics of a classic building. But he was not familiar with gravity fed wineries. Fortunately, McIntyre had been trained in winemaking and knew all about wineries, so he came on as the project's general manager.

That's not to say that the Captain wasn't deeply involved in creating the winery. *His agents throughout Europe continued to send him books* on the latest advances in winemaking methods and technology, and these were incorporated into the building and winery processing.

The Inglenook Winery design was such a success that Hamden McIntyre spent many years designing some of Napa's most famous winery buildings. Considering that Hamden's original training included wooden New England style buildings, it's said that only two of his local redwood wineries remain. The first is the winemaking barn at Frog's Leap in Rutherford, with its jaunty leaping frog weathervane. *Their slogan is, "Time's fun when you're having flies."* The other is the classic, three story Eschol winery, today owned by the Trefethen family, at the corner of Saint Helena Highway and Oak Knoll, surrounded by their five-hundred-acre vineyard.

The story goes that it was McIntyre's favorite and that his ghost haunts it. However, that's pretty unlikely. Not that it's haunted, wine country has plenty of ghosts. But it's not McIntyre, because even though he was in high demand for his winery designs, Hamden and Susan moved back to Vermont where he stayed productive, although not building his wonderful wineries.

If you love buildings, please visit the Trefethen winery, because it is a wonderful example of the New England woodworker's art with its massive beams and classic joints. Another example is the red barn at the Nickel and Nickel property in Oakville. Built in the 1700's, *it was disassembled and transported to the estate where it was carefully reassembled.*

I've walked though many of these classic barns and I thought I knew a bit about them, but then the director of Napa's Historical Society filled in a fascinating connection. The wood joints that hold the classic New England barns together *are the same designs as those used on sailing ships of the period.* How did that happen? Simple, the same craftsman built both barns and ships, moving back and forth between the country and the coast with the seasons.

This combination of well-traveled European investors, sturdy northern Italian stonemasons and a New England winery engineer resulted in a collection of wineries that often resemble fortresses, like Far Niente, Chateau Montelena, Greystone and many more. These grand structures are interspersed with dozens of smaller stone buildings from that period. This was the *last great expression* of the traditional builders' art that had developed over the centuries. As the twentieth century dawned, natural stone was eclipsed by steel, aluminum, plywood and sheet rock.

In 1919 Prohibition began and most of the winery buildings were abandoned. Even though it ended thirteen years later, many growers had shifted to other crops. It wasn't until the 1970s, when there were more orchards than vineyards in the valley, that the interest in growing premium wine grapes locally was revived. That's when investors began looking at these great structures and imagining the possibilities.

One of the hidden advantages that often made the expense of renovation worthwhile was an idiosyncrasy of the winery regulations. It's much easier legally to establish a new winery on a site where a previous one had operated, even if just one corner of that building remains.

When building in California, one must always consider the effects of *earthquakes*, because they will eventually happen! One of the more interesting stories

I heard is about our dear Inglenook. After the devastating 6.9 Loma Prieta earthquake, that shook the 1989 World Series, engineers examined public buildings to determine how to make them safe. They were followed by tradesmen with bolts, straps and steel to stop structures from being knocked off their foundations, or crumbling.

The main building at Inglenook is an impressive pile of stone quarried from the property, along with a significant amount poured concrete. It is three stories tall, sitting on thick walls, cut by narrow windows, with a series of arched chambers on the first floor to store wine barrels.

As is common with gravity fed wineries like Far Niente and Graystone, Inglenook is built into a hillside. That allowed grape wagons to drive up the low hill behind the winery to the level of the very solid second floor. There men would unload bins of grapes into the fermentation tanks. Finally, when the yeast had turned the juice into wine, a hose was attached to the tank and run down to the first floor. They would open the valve and fill the empty aging barrels without needing a pump. This was important in the days before electric and pneumatic pumps were commonplace. In those days moving juice required either a siphon and buckets, or a manual pump with a long handle and a *strong arm*.

Because Inglenook's concrete second story was so substantial, McIntyre knew it made the upper building heavy, so he planned for that. The masons embedded old trolley car cables into the wet concrete of that thick, second floor. The ends were *anchored into the*

Inglenook Winery

hillside, to prevent the earthquakes, that would surely come from breaking up Inglenook's tight embrace of its hillside. Today, the building and grounds enjoy an abundance of care and it's surely worth the visit. As the engineers inspected the building, they were amazed that it didn't suffer any structural damage in the quake."

A *horrible* example of what a quake can do was Trefethen's wooden winery. The 2014 Napa quake happened during harvest, and even though the wooden building no longer operates as a gravity fed winery, they had wine barrels, filled with water, on the second floor preparing to accept new wine. It made the building top heavy enough to magnify the quake's effects.

The result that I saw driving up the valley was a building leaning over about four feet. Those huge one hundred-and twenty-year-old redwood beams had bent but not broken. That great building never let go of its foundation.

Trefethen Family Vineyards

When they started the restoration, they attached cables to the upright beams and anchored them to the foundation at the back of the building. They planned to do a *'chiropractic adjustment,'* cranking the cables tighter and tighter until the building stood straight. They were hoping to get an inch of movement a day, but on the first day those big beams flexed, and the building stood right up, within inches of its original position. After the family's herculean efforts, it is still greeting visitors today.

The Far Niente Winery was built at the same time and also into a small knoll, with two driveways running up the hill to the two upper floors. Today, when you visit the winery, the very top floor is a charming reception area, with a long table for guests and windows that look east over the vineyards. The building was the work of the Italian masons who carved the words *'Far Niente'* into the lintel above the planned cave entrance, that were dug almost ninety years later. Those words are a fragment of the winery's original name, 'In Dolce Far Niente,' which itself is a shortened version of the original Italian expression, "Il dolce piacere per far niente," meaning *the sweet pleasure of doing nothing.*

For men who worked daily with blocks of stone, hammers, chisels and hand cranked cranes, their leisure time must have been especially sweet. The building sat empty for many years, but not entirely due to prohibition. During that unfortunate period when making wine was illegal, a wealthy widow lived in the home with her young and dashing second husband, who had been a World War One flying Ace. He built an *airstrip* on the property and routinely smuggled liquor out of the valley in his airplane. His entrepreneurial venture came to an unfortunate end when his wife's daughter, who had no affection for her stepfather, poisoned him!

After that, the joy pretty much went out of the home, and it sat empty for many years. When the current owners, the Nickel family, took it over in the 1970's they found that the structure was so well built that the main task, prior to installing the new systems, was removing the trees and bushes that had overtaken the property in the ensuing years. *Then they dug the caves.*

Not every stone building from that era was so fortunate. At the top of the valley at the northern edge of the town of Saint Helena, a very long and tall building called Greystone towers over the road. It was once the home of the Christian Brothers Cellars, but thanks to the Loma Prieta earthquake, it is now the west coast home of The Culinary Institute of America.

The Culinary Institute of America at Greystone

Unlike Inglenook and Far Niente, which were built into knolls on the settled valley floor, Greystone was built into an unstable hillside in the narrowest part of the valley. This is where the western slope of the volcanic Vaca Mountains *almost touches* the eastern slope of the Mayacamas Mountains, that in this part of the valley contains a great deal of volcanic ash. The two ranges form a mile wide neck on the bottom-heavy hourglass shape that describes the Napa Valley.

The hillside is so steep that Greystone's parking lot sits high above the road, where a long flight of steep stairs brings you up to the first floor. At the back of that ground floor, Chinese workers had dug a wine cave that went deep into the hillside. Inside the central entranceway, multiple open staircases wind their way up to the top floor where the cooking school now resides. This complex balancing act of leaning against the hill and defying gravity worked well for many years, *until* the Loma Prieta earthquake gave those ashy hillsides a serious shaking.

At the time, the Christian Brothers had been making wine there for many years and aging it in the caves below. As an aside, in case you're wondering whether these are natural caves, while in the long history of winemaking, natural caves have been employed, the caves in the north bay were, and continue to be dug by industrious miners.

After the quake, the inherent instability that existed on that hillside made itself known. It required an extensive amount of work to prevent the building's walls from heading off in different directions. This required the installation of a constellation of *'earthquake stars'* that can be seen on the front of the building. They serve as the end nuts for steel rods that span the building and connect the front and back walls together, preventing them from spreading apart.

The place where this instability was most obvious was in the dirt below, where the cave was located. It was also the place that would be the hardest and most expensive to fix, because there's an awful lot of unstable stone on top of those caves and gravity is undeniable. For the Christian Brothers this was a disaster because having a cool, humid cave to age their wine was essential.

Eventually, Christian Brothers decided to move to another facility and the building was sold to the Culinary Institute of America *for a dollar*, with the acceptance that it was up to the new owners to do the required repairs. Fortunately, the CIA, as it's known locally, was looking for a West Coast location.

Sonoma was also in the running, but the Greystone property was a good solution for them for an odd reason. They were one of the few potential buyers in the heart of Wine Country that wasn't a winery, so they didn't care about the condition of the caves.

While the 'earthquake stars' on the exterior can be mistaken for decorations, inside the north part of the building that is less supported by the hill, there is so much structural steel arching through the rooms that you feel like you're standing inside the upper parts of the Brooklyn Bridge.

That part of the Valley, on the edge of the little town of Saint Helena, is also home to Napa's oldest winery, Charles Krug. It was started on land that was part of his wife's dowry. Charles had worked for the Count over in Sonoma as a winemaker, before he started his own winery, which he owned for a short time. But the ensuing owners built two remarkable stone buildings, one for the winery and an expansive carriage house that today is used for events.

The Mondavi family came north from the Central Valley after WWII and bought the winery and ran it as a family affair. After the famous feud between the two brothers, Robert took his share and started his own winery, and Peter's family has continued to make their wines there in a modern, solar powered building. The historic winery is used for aging barrels and hospitality. One of Krug's employees was fellow Prussian, Jacob Beringer.

While Jacob worked at Krug, his brother in New York was raising money, and eventually they bought the land across the street and started the Beringer Brothers Winery in 1876. The stone winery buildings were tucked against the hill so they could dig caves in the back. Their most remarkable architectural contribution was their Rhine House. To build it Jacob moved a spacious, California style home to the north where it is surrounded by a lovely grove of redwood trees. This way his emblematic building would stand out prominently just inside the gate. The Rhine House was based on their childhood home in Prussia, so the fish and birds portrayed in the stained-glass windows are those breeds found *near their ancestral home*. The dining room windows include food themes, the drawing room tea and beverages.

This impressively beautiful building was one of Napa's first great 'castles'. Today the mansion that was once their home is used for pouring their most expensive wines, while the old winery building is used for the rest of the list. The wines are made across the road, outside in an orderly collection of stainless-steel tanks you can see as you drive by on Saint Helena Highway.

Another contemporary winery in that neighborhood is on the road up to Spring Mountain. It was built buy a *Monsieur Parrot,* the French son of Captain Gustave Niebaum's business partner in their wildly successful shipping company. It includes an impressive hillside cave fronted by a dramatic steeple.

He and his wife were planning their home just after Jacob Beringer had completed his dramatic Rhine House, that was turning everyone's head. For Monsieur and Madame Parrot, it was a daunting task trying to keep up with the Berringer's' love of expensive, decorative woods and stained glass, *so they took a simpler route.* Parrot simply told their architect, 'We don't care what it looks like so much, as long as it's taller than the Beringer's house,' and it is!

In an interesting Hollywood twist, the house was used in the 1980's 'nighttime soap opera' Falcon Crest, about wealthy families of wine country. The intro featured the image of a falcon from one of the house's stained-glass windows. In the true spirit of Hollywood, the part of *the titular Falcon shown in the window, was played by a parrot,* the namesake of the family Parrot!

The same masons that built the wineries laid the blocks and bricks for many of the charming storefront buildings in downtown Saint Helena and Napa. Those materials set them apart from downtown Sonoma on the other side of the Mayacamas Mountains. There you'll find a wonderful collection of adobe buildings constructed during the Spanish colonial period, with their soft, rounded edges, enclosing courtyards and paseos, shielded from the heat. The main reason that Sonoma never replaced the buildings was money, there is no river nearby so there was less commerce. But, because downtown Sonoma lacked a river, they didn't suffer from Napa's devastating floods, so they simply repaired the buildings they had, including the historic Mission and the Presidio Barracks.

In comparison, the Napa River promoted so much commercial activity, and the downtown was so subject to floods, that the owners could afford to tear down the single-story, mud adobes and replace them with more durable, multi-story stone buildings, in the early 1900's. The only historic Napa adobe was beautifully restored and today is home to a restaurant south of downtown Napa. It was the home of the original Mexican settler and his family, Sergeant Nicolás Higuera, who had received a massive land grant from his commander, General Vallejo. His ranchero included what is today downtown Napa and a large part of Los Carneros.

In 2014 the Napa Quake destructively shook the downtown, where massive stone blocks flew off the fronts of the turn of the century buildings. In Sonoma, even though the quake burst the wine tanks at the downtown Sebastiani winery, the historic adobes came through it with just a few cracks. Rebuilding downtown Napa was a lengthy process because those Italian stone masons are long gone, and today fewer people possess those remarkable and enduring skills.

Today the masons are still mostly immigrants, and they continue to build remarkable structures. One of the most beautiful modern wineries in Napa is Darioush. It is constructed from golden travertine marble quarried in Iran and milled and carved in Italy and Turkey. It is patterned on the ancient Persian capital *Persepolis*. I also heard that it was based on *Heliopolis*, the temple of the Sun, which seems suitable considering the material and design.

It is a beautifully balanced building, with a large complex cave underneath. The center front section is for hospitality, while the left wing is their office. The winery is at the back and separated by a glass wall. The right wing is a home. Outside at the north side of the building is an amphitheater, where the upper rows are at ground level, and the bottom is at the same level as the cave floor. The front of the building faces west, but the draining effects of the afternoon sun are mitigated by the rich colors of the materials.

As you approach Darioush columns mimic a line of trees, topped with sculptures of horses. On either side are ponds with water flowers. In the center is a sunken area with steps down to the paved floor. This is a seating area that I've only seen used once. It was filled with low, Persian cushions, and an off-white cloth was draped over the tops of the columns to provide shade, making it an amazingly appealing space.

For all the chateaus, villas and mansions that populate the North Bay, the Castello di Amorosa in Northern Napa has the greatest right to the title, *'Castle,'* because it was patterned on Tuscan Medieval castles. The person who dreamed this up was Dario Sattui, of the long-time V. Sattui Winery. Thanks to its location in a commercial zone, instead of the restrictive Agricultural Preserve, V. Sattui is able to have a deli with picnic tables. When I started wine touring in 2005, one out of every eight Napa visitors tasted at V. Sattui and then had lunch there.

After a good run Dario was semi-retired, spending half his time in Italy. But back in Napa Valley he bought a hillside vineyard behind a large house just south of downtown Calistoga that he planned to turn into a Bed and Breakfast. The next part of the story is a bit of my speculation about how the idea for a castle winery in Napa came about. About the time when he was living in Tuscany, a local family was building a winery styled as a castle. You could see it from the Autostrada, along with a very tall, turquoise crane.

The idea of creating a destination winery in Tuscany was quite a departure. Italy has half a million wineries and the place is practically carpeted in vineyards, so having a winery in your neighborhood is about as common as having a bakery. It must have got Dario thinking, "If they can build a castle winery in Tuscany, why can't I build one in Napa?" so he did!

He had architects create plans of various Tuscan castles and then they got together and created a new design. They built an authentic hundred and seven room, eight level high stone castle, using tons of building materials, including wrought iron and carvings from Italy.

He named it Castello Di Amorosa, or 'Castle of the Beloved.' Was it a good bet? I was there two weeks after it opened, when I hadn't seen a single advertisement for it yet, and they were already *booked to capacity*. Another time I dropped by with my daughter and Disney was shooting the movie 'Bedtime Story' starring Adam Sandler.

For that they finally filled the moat with water and in return the crew built an impressive Medieval village that extended from the front path to the drawbridge and into the courtyard. But even during filming, the tasting room downstairs stayed open.

El Castello is *one of three destination wineries within sight of its parapets.* The original star of the upper valley was Sterling, opening their white, Greek, Mykonos Island style winery on the top of a hill in the 1970's. It features a tramway to carry visitors from the parking lot up to the winery with its splendid views. Sterling was the first winery to charge for tastings, although you could say that the guests paid for the tram ride, and once they arrived at the top the wines were free.

Just across the street from the entrance to Sterling is Clos Pegase. Traditionally, Clo in the name of a French winery means a walled, or enclosed vineyard. Clo Pegase was originally home to a wonderful sculpture collection, inside of a *delightfully colorful Michael Graves designed building.* Being able to taste their wines while surrounded by this wonderful collection of art was a unique experience. Periodically they had artists in residence who would use the tank room as their studio and gallery. But things change. Clos Pegase was sold, and the art collection departed with the owner.

For some unknown and ill-informed reason, the new *owners painted that beautiful, uniquely colored building a remarkably boring gray.* So, while Clo Pegase continues to make good wines, the draw for art and architecture is gone.

Then, in 2020 the North Napa fire burned massive tracts above downtown Saint Helena, forcing part of the town's evacuation. The fire raged up Howell

Mountain and the firebrands blew across the valley onto Spring Mountain. The fires destroyed dozens of winery buildings, homes and even some steep hillside vineyards. While most of the vineyards weren't touched by the fires, smoke damage tainted the grapes still on the vines so badly that they became unusable. *The fire climbed Sterling's steep hilltop,* destroying many of the trees that had once shaded the buildings and leaving burn marks on the outside of the winery.

Fortunately, it did not go up in flames, although it destroyed the popular tramway, which was the only way to bring customers to the top. It took until October of 2023 for Sterling to reopen. After being part of a dynamic trio of destination wineries at the top of the valley, suddenly the Castello found itself the sole star in that constellation. That was true even though the hills surrounding it were covered with charred tree stumps, and their large storage building, filled with wine, was gutted by the fire. However, they got their doors open to visitors after that disaster remarkably fast. There is an advantage to being in a traditional stone building.

From the road El Castello sits hidden, on the far side of an impressive gate, up a long, steep, curving lane lined with trees and vines. As you approach, the building suddenly appears, a towering pile of stone at the top of the hill. An orchard of hundred-year-old Italian olive trees, and grazing sheep surround the building. The architecture includes some whimsical grace notes. A favorite of mine are the small 'repair' bricks that were fit into 'damaged' addition that juts out over the eastern entrance to the cellar. There are also the bricked up 'old' doorways and crumbling towers that you expect to see in a Medieval Castle. It makes the statement that, *'Yes, we've taken hits and it's been hard, but we adapted to the times, and we are still here!'*

Castello di Amorosa

Chapter Eight
Sonoma and Napa, Ancient Siblings

Understanding the relationship between Sonoma and Napa is like recognizing the connections between siblings. I imagine Sonoma as the older sister, dark-haired, good looking, industrious, a great cook and gardener and always responsible. Meanwhile, Napa is her golden-haired little brother that everyone makes a fuss over. Whenever he shows up carrying a basket of grapes, or a bottle of wine, everybody turns around and looks at him smiling. It drives his older sister crazy, even though she knows that he adores her.

People visiting often assume there must be competition between the two regions. After all, these are *two of the world's most popular wine destinations* with respected international reputations and markets. A big part of their tourism success *stems from them being conveniently close to San Francisco,* itself a long-time tourist and convention destination. Because the North Bay Wine Country was a popular day trip from the city, their fame spread until they eventually became destinations themselves.

Surprisingly, there's little competition between the two, although maybe a little friendly rivalry, for a very good reason. Even though they are both wine growing regions, they produce wines from mostly different grapes. That is a function, as is always the case in natural agriculture, of location. California's western border is the Pacific Ocean, and that massive body of frigid water shapes almost everything about grape growing in the state.

The closer you are to the ocean, the cooler the temperatures. Because the North Bay wine region is divided up by hills and mountains, running north to south, *each valley you cross, going east from the ocean, is warmer.* There are thousands of grape varieties world-wide, and they all have specific climates to which they are most adapted, so as you travel east from Sonoma to Napa, the varieties that thrive change.

There is no ignoring the reality that the two countries that most influenced winemaking in California are France and Italy. But here we come to a paradox. The most popular, successful and prestigious wines made in California come from grapes that originated in France. Yet, much of the labor and entrepreneurship that created the wine industry in America came from Italian immigrants. They initially planted vines that produced wines that tasted familiar and coincidentally, ripened early, such as Zinfandel, originally from Croatia, Grenache, from Spain via southern France, and the French varietals Alicante Bouchet and Petite Sirah. Over time, their popularity was supplanted by the French Chardonnay and Cabernet Sauvignon, the world's two most widely planted premium grapes. In Napa and Sonoma, where they grow California's most expensive wines knowing what to plant can be challenging.

Because it takes so long for the vines to mature and produce good grapes, growers need to forecast the market, and that means taking risks. But farmers are typically risk *averse*, which makes them resistant to change. You can always tell the serious grape growers in the area by their gray hair, from worrying about what the weather gods are going to do to their vines each year. The barometer they often watch are the grape varietals that are selling well in the fine restaurants, where many customers first encounter premium wines, because that's what they will look for in the future!

In France, Chardonnay and Pinot Noir are grown in the cool northeast regions of Burgundy and Champagne. Cabernet blends are grown in the warmer southwest region of Bordeaux. north of the San Francisco Bay, the relationship between France's northeast and southwest becomes the difference between cool Western Sonoma and warm Eastern Napa. While Burgundy and Bordeaux are hundreds of miles apart, the ride from Sonoma to Napa is just a twenty-minute drive over the wooded

Mayacamas Mountains. There is a California saying that is a truism, *"If you don't like the weather, just drive twenty minutes."*

Sonoma is almost three times larger than Napa and the two are topographically separated by the broad Mayacamas Mountains. There is only one relatively level road connecting them. It's called the Carneros Highway, and it stretches across the rolling hills just north of San Pablo Bay, which is what they call the northern reaches of the San Francisco Bay. Most of the road is wonderfully flat, except for *one big hill* at the county line. That steep ridge is the southernmost tip of the Mayacamas Mountains.

Today, for the modern traveler in an air-conditioned car listening to their music, the crest of the hill is a pleasant announcement that they've arrived in the next county, but in the days of *horse drawn wagons, teamsters surely dreaded that climb.* They couldn't build the road further south, where the land is flatter, because it would have skirted the malarial marshes and been prone to flooding. Further to the west in Sonoma the lower part of the road often floods in the Winter, even though the border of the bay has been pushed back behind grasslands protected by levies.

Napa is one wide valley, with vineyards carpeting the floor in some places and then extending up into the surrounding hills and canyons. Sonoma is made up of numerous valleys, large and small, that each create their own unique climates. Sonoma vineyards tend to be tucked in between forests, orchards, farms and towns.

To the west of the Sonoma Valley, over a low line of hills, alongside a river is the cooler, and very hip town of Petaluma. *The name means 'low hills' in the native language.* That small distance makes a difference. Sitting in the Sonoma Plaza on a bright morning with a cup of coffee, we would often see clouds hanging in the west, and comment, "Ah, it's cloudy in Petaluma." Whenever we drive there it's not quite as bright and warm as downtown Sonoma.

Farther west, beyond a wide plain, is the final line of steep hills beyond which are the cool waters of the Pacific. This is Sonoma's coastal region where they grow many of the most prized pinot noir grapes, and graze cattle on hills that stay green through much of the year.

Sonoma, with its complex geology and multitude of climates, can successfully grow a wider selection of grapes than Napa. While it's most famous for Pinot Noir and Chardonnay from the Russian River Valley and Los Carneros, it shines in other areas too.

Sonoma Valley, which thanks to its proximity to San Francisco, has long been a popular tourist destination, is a magical place that seems to be able to do a good job of growing every kind of local grape well. *Little Bennett Valley, which branches off to the west from the Sonoma Valley, produces some of the state's best Syrah.*

Northern Sonoma's Dry Creek Valley is famous for its Zinfandel. Next door, the Alexander Valley, with its broad floor at the foot of the eastern slopes of the Mayacamas Mountains, enjoys big sun and cool nights, much like Napa. Alexander Valley grows similar varietals on a different geology, so their Merlot is more muscular, and the Cabernet Sauvignon is milder. This is the home of *Geyser Peak,* that for years spewed steam from its cone. This area was actively volcanic ten thousand years ago, not long in geological time. It makes the charming town of Geyserville subject to daily, but minor tremors. Being in this perpetual state of flux gives it the feeling of a dusty old western town, that happens to have great restaurants, cool tasting rooms and a friendly cafe.

Unlike so many Spanish named cities in California, Sonoma and Napa's names spring from the native languages. This speaks volumes about the prosperity of this place where the native tongues had no word for starvation. The region directly north of the bay is one of the longest continually inhabited regions in North America, and that continuity promotes great culture. *The Sonoma tribes were famous storytellers and revered for their knowledge of plants. The Napa tribes were skilled craftspeople and their obsidian knives,* arrowheads and grinding boards were valuable assets to tribes throughout the west.

In the traditions of exploration, the fact that Sonoma was developed before Napa is an anomaly. Napa has the great advantage of being accessible by a navigable river, which should have tilted the odds in their favor. But the Spanish empire's resources were stretched to the breaking point in the 1800's, and they didn't have ships to spare for exploring the bay's complex network of rivers. That's because their galleons were sailing from the coast of Mexico, on the prevailing southern currents, *across the Pacific to the Philippines for the very profitable spice trade.* On their return, riding the northern currents, they would make landfall on the Alta California coast, and then follow that south to their base in Mexico. They would stay far out to sea to avoid the fog and the treacherous currents along the shore. With so much wealth at stake they wouldn't risk their cargo just to explore some wild place at the ends of the Earth.

While the Commandant in Monterey didn't have command of ships, he did have soldiers and horses. So, the way that the Spanish reached Sonoma was by crossing the Golden Gate inlet in boats and walking north for several days. The other route that they used when moving horses required a long ride east, staying south of the marshes, to where they could ford the Sacramento River, followed by a long ride west to Sonoma.

On the eve of the Bear Flag Rebellion in 1846, when California declared itself an independent Republic on the Sonoma Plaza in front of the barracks, this route played a critical role. When the Bear Flaggers arrived in Sonoma the General had no soldiers handy to confront them. He had sent them to escort a herd of horses to the Governor, his nephew, in Monterey, via the Sacramento River route!

The soldiers had camped for the night in the hills of southeastern Napa. In the morning, while they were having breakfast, a troop of mounted Bear Flaggers charged into the camp, with their guns out and ready.

They told the young lieutenant to continue on to Monterey and to inform the Governor that *they were taking command of Sonoma,* and oh, by the way, they were taking the herd of horses too! The lieutenant objected, saying that they never would have overcome his men if they had been prepared for the horsemen. The American leader of the horsemen, who was known for his propensity for violence, and for continually smelling of liquor said, *"No problem. We'll ride out and give you a chance to get ready, and then ride back in again."* Faced with that unappealing prospect, the lieutenant withdrew his objection, relinquished the herd and continued on to Monterey with the message.

The Bear Flaggers were due in Sonoma the next day, and they realized that moving the herd would take more time than they had, so they left the horses in the little valley, planning to return for them later. It seems like that didn't work out as planned, because today that remote area came to be called Wild Horse Valley.

But before the Bear Flaggers raised their banner on the plaza, Sonoma served as the northern most Franciscan Mission, Imperial Spanish Military base, and an official city, or pueblo, complete with a court, judge and records. Sonoma was also settled first because while the native tribes of Sonoma were no pushovers, the Wappo tribe of Napa was *terrifying*. The name comes from the Spanish, 'Guapo,' or 'brave,' which morphed into 'Wappo.'

Their fierce resistance survived the Spanish and the Mexicans, and it was finally the United States Cavalry, battle hardened by the Civil War, who moved the surviving women, children and old men to a coastal reservation, or Rancheria. Most of the braves had been killed in the years of conflict.

The wide variety of grapes grown in Sonoma is different from very focused Napa, where half of the vineyards are Cabernet Sauvignon and most of the rest are its blending grapes: Merlot, Cabernet Franc, Malbec and Petite Verdot. The old Italian American families in Northern Napa grow a fair amount of Zinfandel vines, which lack trellises and instead look like small bushes. In the cool, southern Carneros region along the bay, Chardonnay and Pinot Noir vineyards abound, along with a small amount of Syrah and even Gamay.

In Sonoma, the last time I checked, they grew more than *100 different varieties*. This incredible diversity comes from several factors. Sonoma is almost three times as large as Napa with a much wider variety of climates and soil types that can support a wider selection of wine grapes. Also, the Italian winemaking tradition makes wines for every palate. When they came to America, they saw no reason to change.

While Napa has a mix of American, French, German and Italian winemaking traditions, Sonoma was dominated by immigrant northern Italian families, because the region is similar to *foggy* Piedmonte. Finally, Sonoma is populated in part by the artists and hippies from San Francisco who made their money and moved north. They are innovative and creative and willing to take risks by making wines from 'out of the box' grapes.

In Sonoma, *quality of life* has always mattered more than prestige, whereas Napa is the reverse. People move to Napa because they want to be noticed for their work and success. A large part of Sonoma is called the Redwood Empire with its heavily forested hills. Because it's closer to the ocean, it's green and wet so in many parts of the county you could build a large estate and once the moving trucks leave, your privacy is assured. Even during the time of the native people, Sonoma has been more eclectic and tribal, with fifty or sixty small villages, each having their own language. In Napa, the fierce but insular Wappo tribe dominated the northern valley, while the larger, more social Patwin tribe, whose territory extended over the eastern hills, harvested fish and seafood in the south along the bay.

Those trends are still true. Napa is divided between the upper valley growers and the down valley businesspeople. Sonoma is made up of numerous eclectic communities spread around a big county with very different priorities. You can spot kids who grew up in Napa because they're very motivated for success. The kids from Sonoma are smart and creative, but value privacy. That may be a little oversimplified, but it's mostly true!

Napa growers focus on Cabernet Sauvignon because they can, thanks to the valley's unique terroir, a French word that describes the mix of climate, location, geology and soil vitality. The Cab vines produce more high-quality fruit on less land than most other varietals, and the grapes command the best prices from the wineries. While their thick skins are resistant to bugs and rain, that toughness means they need very bright sunlight, warm days and a long growing season to ripen completely.

They also need cool nights to shut down their metabolism, so the fruit maintains its acid levels and rich flavors.

These conditions are found in great wine regions globally, and Napa's weather produces it consistently. It has made these vineyards California's *most expensive*, on par with the best of France and Italy. Is it any surprise that locally they have a saying, 'Cabernet is King?' But if that is true then Merlot is Queen, because that juicy likable grape shows up in so many blends.

There is another, very obstructive reason the two counties are not traditionally competitive with each other. That's the big line of mountains that rise up between the two counties. They are called the Mayacamas which in the native tongue means 'many springs.' That remarkable geological feature is part of the secret success of this region. Wine grapes like it dry and this region can go for six months without significant rain, which coincides with the vine's growing cycle. But between the underground springs and overnight fog the vines get the water they need in a form that doesn't promote the biggest threat to grapes, mold and fungus.

The Mayacamas have been a practical obstruction since the days of horse drawn wagons. Family grape growers and winery owners by necessity form long term relationships, often intermarrying. So, for many years the winemakers only tended to buy grapes from the easier to reach vineyards to the north and south before they looked for fruit across the mountains.

Sonoma buys from Mendocino County which sits to the north, known for grapes and cannabis, and Marin

County to the south with their cool weather grapes and great shopping. It is also the way to San Francisco over the Golden Gate Bridge. Napa buys from Lake County, a big growing area to the north and Solano County to the east and south, which provides less expensive grapes and a route to San Francisco over the Bay Bridge.

A story that perfectly describes this dilemma goes back to the early 1970's when Mike Grgich needed chardonnay grapes for Chateau Montelena in Northern Napa. He went to Northern Sonoma to the Bacigalupi family vineyards to get the quality he wanted. The only truck that Charles and Helen Bacigalupi had was a very *underpowered* VW, a version of the iconic van with a truck back. The mountains that separate the vineyards and the winery are high and steep. Helen had to get a running start to make it over the crest, hoping the whole time that no one slower got in her way, because she would lose her precious momentum.

Thanks to bigger, more muscular trucks it's common for Napa and Sonoma wineries to purchase grapes from each other, especially Pinot Noir from the Russian River, and less often Cabernet from Napa, because Cab is so expensive. Like I said, Napa adores his older sister, but in response sometimes Sonoma *just rolls her eyes!*

Chapter Nine
Who Named Mount Saint Helena?

How Mount Saint Helena got her name is a favorite story of ours, because it's adventurous, romantic, and connects the two regions. This very pretty mountain stands at the northern border of Sonoma and Napa, standing just under five thousand feet tall, and looking like *the volcanic cone that she was three million years ago*. Many new visitors to the West Coast, when they first hear the name, confuse this with Mount Saint Helens, the volcano in Washington State that famously erupted in 1980. People are horrible at geography! Saint Helena, in comparison, is about three thousand feet smaller. She's more of a 'designer mountain,' good looking, graceful and accessible.

She does have warm feet, because thermal tubes from more recent volcanos to the north pass under her skirts. Those tubes provide the heat for the popular hot springs that boil to the surface in the town of Calistoga. Sam Brannan, who founded the town in the mid-1800's, claimed it would be the "Saratoga Springs of California." Sam inadvertently named the town when, during a brandy-soaked event for his investors at his hot springs spa, his inebriated tongue claimed it would be "The Calistoga of Sarafornia!" Of course, in a town with such a good sense of humor, there is a *Café Sarafornia*.

While Mount Saint Helena looks like a volcanic cone from the Napa Valley floor, when you see her from Northern Sonoma, sailing over the ridges of the Mayacamas mountain range that separates the two counties, she appears as a rambling series of descending mounds *in the shape of a woman's body*. That distinctive shape is part of one of the stories behind the naming of the mountain. This is the quintessential example of a wine country story because there are at least four versions that all sound mostly feasible. Which story you hear depends on where you are and who is telling it, and how much wine has been consumed.

Not surprisingly, you'll hear different versions of the story in Napa and Sonoma. In Napa, the story goes that the mountain was named by a Russian Princess who climbed the mountain in the 1800's. Many people don't realize that while Northern California was the northern tip of the Spanish empire, it was also the southern tip of the Russian Empire's reach in the Americas. The icy Russian seal hunting camps in Alaska needed provisions and they saw the temperate Sonoma coast as the solution. Princess Elena, her husband and three children were in the party that traveled in two ships to Sonoma where they established a farming community. Compared to frozen Alaska, this slice of the coast was a little piece of heaven, where the fields for grazing livestock stayed green most of the year, and everything they planted quickly sprouted and prospered.

The locals called it Fort Ross, or 'Rooss,' or 'Rossiya', for Mother Russia. Considering *the diverse languages spoken in the area; Spanish, English, Russian, Polish, Chinese, Kodiak, Pomo, Patwin and Onasai,* it's amazing that the name stayed that close to the original. While that explains how the Russian River Valley got its name, it still seems strange that a Princess would find herself on the far ends of the Earth and have the opportunity to name a mountain.

The story I heard was that the Princess Elena Pavlovna Gagarina, *the niece of the Czarina and an exceptionally beautiful young woman, fell in love with a handsome Count.* He was brave, resourceful and a renowned poet. But Alexander Rotchev's rank was many steps below that of his beloved Elena. In the Russian Court rank mattered, so not surprisingly, the Czarina did not give her blessing for the marriage. Elena followed her heart and they married anyway. Amazingly, the Count's opportunities dried up. After a long wait, he was offered a posting at the camp in Alaska, the farthest and coldest reaches of the Russian Empire. Here's an important lesson, when someone holds your fate in their hands, don't piss off the Czarina! So, the Count bundled his wife and their young children, off to the ends of the Earth.

Fortunately for the young couple, the governor of Alaska saw Alexander as a man he could trust to accomplish a difficult venture. He also probably felt sorry for this sophisticated, young family struggling in the frozen wasteland. So, he assigned Alexander to take those two ships, and his family, and sail south along the coast to establish a farming community.

It had to be done carefully because the British had claimed the coast of Canada. Further south, New England sea captains held sway over what is today Washington and Oregon and dominated shipping along the Pacific Coast. They originally ventured there to hunt whales, but then found a profitable living transporting finished products from the New England workshops and factories to the settlers and gold miners.

On Spain Street in downtown Sonoma is a pretty, Victorian house that is home to a restaurant called the General's Daughter. It was built in New England and transported in pieces in the belly of a sailing ship for General Vallejo as a wedding gift for one of his daughters. His own house, built in the same New England workshops, is a short walk away. It sits below the 'Lachryma Montis' springs, the 'tears of the mountain.' That was also the name of Vallejo's wine brand when he was one of the biggest producers in the North Bay.

The Russians couldn't travel far south without

upsetting the Spanish Governor, who resided in Monterey, and who had a small garrison on the San Francisco Bay. The Spanish considered 'Alta California', as it was known, a wild place. Their settlements there probably only developed due to the spice trade. The Galleons, returning from the Philippines rode the circular Pacific currents. Their first landfall was normally along the Northern California coast. As they made their way south at about six knots, they explored the coast looking for bays where they could moor and take on fresh water and provisions. One of the first bays they discovered was Carmel and that became the home of the first Northern California Franciscan Mission.

So as Alexander and Elena sailed south, they had to find a spot that the English, Americans and Spaniards were not interested in. They settled on a piece of the California coast just north of the Russian River delta. While the river is too shallow for a ship, it was perfect for the sturdy Aleut hunters and their kayaks, which they brought along on their incessant search for furs. To say this spot, covered with towering redwood forests, was remote is an understatement. It was the middle of nowhere! Even today, with good roads and driving in a car it's a hike!

Because Northern California was so difficult to reach, it was a land of brave and capable adventurers, and its fair share of fools. Imagine the splash it created to have this brilliant and sophisticated couple arrive in their midst. That Elena was a true blonde beauty, certainly turned many heads in this land that was populated by dark haired Spaniards and native tribes. Despite the Fort's remote location, the Princess and the Count hosted local dignitaries including General Vallejo and his ally, Chief Solano.

They in turn were welcomed at the General's home in Sonoma. The fact that Mariano Guadalupe Vallejo had been sent north to keep the Russians from expanding their operations to the south seems to have been temporarily forgotten. That is not surprising. *This charming couple, who were so obviously in love,* brought some very appreciated glamour and sophistication to this rustic place. From Mariano's point of view, they were a wonderful addition, and Mexico City was very far away.

Princess Elena and her husband Alexander were the last directors of Russia's settlement in California. Well before the Czar's final days, seventy years later, they abandoned it because of increasing pressure from the Americans who were flooding the area. Here we get to the first two stories about the naming of Mount Saint Helena. Before they left, Elena, or 'Helena' took the opportunity to travel throughout the area with two Russian scientists who were recording their observations of the area. Of course, they brought along some hardy helpers with rifles because this area had a lively community of fierce braves and California Grizzly Bears.

From Sonoma they could see Mount Mayacamas, as the natives called Mount Saint Helena, towering over the mountain ridge to the east. Elena, with the scientists and bodyguards, trekked over the hills and climbed the almost 5,000-foot peak. She was clearly a very vigorous woman because it's quite a climb. The name was changed from Mayacamas, which meant 'many springs,' when the climbing party installed a bronze plaque at the peak declaring it to be Mount Saint Helena and including the names of various Russian dignitaries.

The name Elena is a variation of Helena, Ilona and Helen. In Napa, the story goes that it was named for Princess Elena. The second variation was that Princess Elena named it for the Czarina's patron Saint, 'Helena,' the mother of the Roman Emperor Constantine, who was the Pontifex Maximus of the Roman Church and coincidentally a famous Astrologer. It was Mama Helena who convinced her son to make Christianity the Empire's official religion. *As the mother of Russia, it was natural that Czarina Alexandra's patron Saint* would be the Emperor's mother who changed the Christian world.

One could imagine that Princess Elena, a sophisticated young woman *banished to the far reaches of the Earth,* wanted to get back in the Czarina's good graces, and return to the comforts of the royal court. We can also imagine her writing the Czarina a letter in her beautiful Cyrillic hand, "Dear Auntie Alexandra, I've named a beautiful mountain for your favorite Saint, can I come home now, please?" and then sealing the letter with wax, a prayer and a tear.

It was not long after the naming of the mountain that the Russians gave up their 'Fort' on the Sonoma coast. Did she and her husband return home to the Russian Court, or did they make their way in California? No one seems to know. Hopefully, their future was as interesting as their past.

There is a second, more romantic version of this story. In that one, Count Alexander and a party of scientists climbed the mountain and installed the plaque. The Helena he was thinking about was his beloved wife Elena, the mother of his children, who had followed him to the ends of the Earth for love.

Now, if you are in Sonoma, the naming of Mount Saint Helena is a different tale. When you see the mountain from the Santa Rosa plains, it's even more impressive than the solitary cone you see from southern Napa. In Sonoma it becomes a long, rambling mountain ridge. In an area where the hills stand between 1,000 and 2,000 feet, Mount Saint Helena, at just under 5000 feet can be seen for many miles around. I heard this story of the naming of Mount Saint Helena from an archaeologist at Fort Ross, so I would normally give it a bit more credence than I give to other wine country stories I've heard.

That's because the stories you hear in Wine Country often benefit from artistic additions, inspired by both the storyteller and the audience being under the influence of some wonderful wines. Our stories are a perfect example of that! With that said, there are some other factors that cast some doubt on this source for the name.

According to my friend at Fort Ross, the mountain was already called Mount Saint Helena before Elena, or Alexander climbed the mountain with their plaque. In this story, the Mountain was first named by the Franciscan missionary, Altamira, who saw it from, what is today, Santa Rosa, which has the distinction of being the Northern most major California city with a Spanish name. Naming every place after Saints, or Angels was normal. Santa Rosa gets its name from 'Saint Rose of Lima,' the first Saint of the Americas.

The story goes that the shape of Saint Helena, which resembles a reclining woman, reminded Altamira of a funerary statue in a church in France. The Patron Saint of the church was Saint Helena. While being named by one of the Franciscan missionaries is always historically notable, this particular Franciscan's history in Northern California is so checkered and vainglorious that it makes you wonder, whether his story about naming the mountain was true.

We know that he established the Sonoma Mission at Los Carneros, close to the bay, *because he was very wary of the tribes to the north* that he would encounter on the way to Santa Rosa.

While the Governor in Monterey had given him soldiers to help, it was a small contingent and Altamira was famously unpopular with the local tribes. In any case, what are the chances that he traveled up the Sonoma Valley to where he could see the mountain? It is more likely that he received descriptions of the mountain from soldiers and recorded the name on a map! *But did he name it, or was he told the name and wove a good story to give himself the credit?*

Cartography is an interesting profession. Here is an interesting fact that is possibly not taught in schools anymore. The way the Americas got their name was because one of the first popular maps of the Americas was based on charts provided by Amerigo Vespucci.

    He signed his name very prominently on the unexplored landmass beyond the coastline, so the mapmakers assumed that was its name. Later when they realized their mistake they changed it on later maps, depending on which countries claimed the various parts of the coast, but the name stuck. Amerigo does have the distinction of being the first person to postulate that this was an entirely different continent, and not part of Asia, as had been previously assumed.

    The adventures of the Franciscan Missionaries north of the bay were short-lived. Eight years after the Sonoma Mission was established under Imperial Mexico, the Mexican Revolution happened and the leaders in Mexico City considered the church an agent of the aristocracy. Any native-born Spaniards, who had not become citizens of Mexico, were forced out and Padre Altamira was sent packing back to Barcelona and was never heard from again. The missions were secularized and the mission buildings on the Sonoma Plaza became General Vallejo's property.

    Like so many Sonoma buildings on the Plaza, the San Francisco Solano Mission survived because they could not afford to replace it. Its sister Mission to the south in San Rafael was taken down when they built a very impressive Spanish style church. Years later, when a group wanted to build a re-creation of the mission building, they had no record of what it looked like. So, they built it using an image found on a popular set of postcards. One slight problem! The publishing company didn't know what the building looked like either. So, they substituted a different view of the very pretty Carmel mission, which had survived nicely.

One More Story

Now those are the first three stories about the naming of Mount Saint Helena, and I promised you four. While you can see Saint Helena from Sonoma, she is very much Napa's Mountain. The town of Napa was founded at the northernmost point that can be reached with a sailing ship so many of Napa's earliest investors were sea captains. The Mexicans didn't prefer Napa for two reasons. First, it's much drier than Sonoma, and second, it was inhabited by the fierce Onasai/Wappo tribe and a multitude of giant California Grizzly bears. *It was much safer to stay in Sonoma!*

But many of the Americans who settled in Napa were sailors, soldiers, military men, mountain men and wagon train leaders. They were adventurous and accustomed to dealing with trouble.

To provide a little context, let's mention that when California became part of the United States, the Presidio at Sonoma became the central Fort for Northern California. Many of the famous Civil War Generals visited the area and the famous General Hooker, whose exploits are well recorded, lived in Sonoma for many years. Today there is a nearby creek named for him and his home, which is just off the Sonoma Plaza, serves as the local Historical Society. There is an old story that the term "Hooker" comes from the numerous 'loose women' that frequented his headquarters. Ever since his service in the Mexican American war there were always ladies around who admired the 'Handsome General." *As the Army moved from camp to camp, they became known as Hooker's Girls.* While the term hooker did appear in print in the years before the General came to prominence, his tendency to run a camp that other officers described as part bar and part brothel, surely helped to make the term more popular.

But back to the story! In Napa, it was the ship captains who left their mark, and their homes, alongside the river. With many of them being New Englanders, they favored Victorian-style homes, but with a California flair. As word of Napa's beautiful, fertile valley and easy access to the bay spread among the sea going community, it attracted more sailors. One of them was *a sea captain from England. He arrived with a purse full of money after a successful trip* and went looking for land in Napa. An adventurous soul looking for a good deal, the captain looked in the far north end of the valley, finally buying a large piece of land that included Mount Saint Helena.

As he stood atop this grand mountain and looked out over the beautiful valley, he realized it was his mountain to name. So, he named it after the ship that had brought him to San Francisco and provided the wealth he needed to make a home in this American Eden. The name of that ship was the 'Saint Helena.' Was it just a coincidence? Did he arrive and find that the mountain had the same name as his ship? Sailors are a superstitious lot, and he could have taken that as a lucky sign! Of course, with time and enough good bottles of wine and brandy, the story more than likely evolved until it was the Captain that coined the name for his pretty little mountain, sitting at the top of a gorgeous valley, north of the San Francisco Bay.

I am not sure which of these stories is true, although *I expect that there's some truth here and there, in bits and pieces.* The one thing that I do know is true and obvious, Mount Saint Helena knew what she wanted to be called.

Afterthought, the Fans

Move To a Vineyard, It Will Be Romantic...!

As we said, we got into the winery tour business quite by accident. We had attended a conference in San Francisco 18 months before and stayed on for a sorely needed vacation. The idea of writing a book about winery buildings from a Feng Shui perspective was the project that inspired us to move 3,000 miles from Philadelphia to Wine Country. It had only taken us 18 months to wrap up the ongoing certification classes we were teaching and figure out the logistics of this coast-to-coast move. Once we settled in, we started our research. It was a fun process because we were, after all, in Wine Country, and we already had a great deal of interest, and a little knowledge about wine. As we made personal connections with a few winemakers and winery owners, our 'buildings book' idea took shape.

We *first* moved to Sonoma for our research and Ralph was out every few days visiting wineries, meeting key people, photographing buildings and developing content. Winery people are a chatty bunch, and they love the idea of inspiring a book. In addition to winemakers and owners, he ran into more than a few tour guides. Then he got the brilliant idea to take a part time job driving wine tours. Why not get paid for a little on-the-job research?

This smart move got him *up close and personal* at a huge number of wineries, talking to people who were grateful for the customers he brought. In the course of his interviews, a secondary theme began to evolve. These winery folks were asking for a 'connect-the-dots' type of tour book to answer visitors' questions about where to eat, where to stay, which winery would they recommend and more. Now, Ralph has a great feel for sales and can't ignore the interests of the 'marketplace.'

As the 'building book' *morphed* into a tour book, we became more and more connected with hotels and wineries, especially in Napa. When opportunities opened up there, we realized it was time to move closer to our connections. Friends suggested different areas and options in Napa, and all of them were very close to the vineyards, something we did not have nearby in Sonoma.

How cool would that be? Living a stone's throw from the wineries that Ralph was visiting with his guests. *"Move to a vineyard,"* they said. *"It will be romantic,"* they said. After an extensive search, we moved in July and found an idyllic spot near the Oak Knoll AVA with beautiful vineyards and wineries a block away. Perfect...!

Fast forward to a Winter night in late March, cozy in our bed at 3AM, when suddenly we hear what could only be a *'bevy of helicopters'* hunting down a crime suspect in our quiet little part of paradise. We say 'bevy' because we were used to the occasional copter in the middle of the night due to being close to a hospital with an emergency helipad. "What is going on?" The sound sort of came and went, like waves of aircraft heading to the west. Could they be squadrons from Travis Air Force Base? If so, something big was happening.

"Turn on the air cleaner... where are my ear plugs... no, throw on some clothes, we have to go out and get to the *bottom* of this." By this time, it was 5 am. "I'll buy you a Starbucks! We have to see what's going on."

If you have been to Wine Country, you may have noticed those big fan-looking things in the middle of some vineyards. We encountered them in Sonoma and when we asked, they said, "Oh, those are frost fans, but they aren't really used anymore." Well, maybe not in Sonoma but they are everywhere in frostier Napa. And when overnight temps get close to freezing around the time of bud break, they certainly use them.

Wineries will not let a whole vineyard of expensive Cabernet vines freeze-dry before they can make their expensive wine. The noisy motors are droning enough, but they also oscillate, adding to that whirring sound that left our brains buzzing.

You know how people have that pet that destroys everything, or yips incessantly and you often wonder, 'Why do they keep that pet?" Well, we understand why now, because we still live in paradise in ear shot of the fans, and we know where they keep the ear plugs at the local Orchard Supply store. And now we know why they carry so many.

We hope you enjoy this book as much as we have enjoyed writing it. And come visit us out here in Wine Country!

Lahni & Ralph DeAmicis found their way from speaking and writing about design and health into also speaking and writing about Wine Country, by starting to write a book about winery buildings. As they researched the topic, they realized there were no local 'winery' tour books, so the project morphed into their first guidebook. That series, now in its seventh edition, continues to be the region's most popular.

Eventually they started Amicis Tours which has taken them, and their clients, to many beautiful places and opened doors for them into the wine industry. Their TV show 'Wine Country at Work' and their documentary film series explore this fascinating region. They share stories about the region with visiting groups. They also do speeches and team building about using the Power of ErgoDynamic Design to improve lives and work performance, with an admittedly Wine Country filter.

www.SpaceAndTime.com

Other Titles by The Authors

A Tour Guide's Napa Valley
A Tour Guide's Sonoma Wine Country
Sonoma Navigator, Maps & Highlights
Napa Navigator, Maps & Highlights
Napa Valley Winery Maps
Sonoma Winery Maps

PlanetaryCalendar.com
Published Annually since 1949

Planetary Calendar Astrology Forecasts & Health Hints
Two Wall Sizes, a Pocket Size, a Day Planner &
a Digital Version for your Phone and Computer
The Lunar Food and Wine Tasting Calendar
The Companion Book
'Planetary Calendar Astrology,
Moving Beyond Observation to Action'
Coming Soon
Reclaiming Astrology from the Patriarchy
The Story of the Stolen Zodiac

From the 'Tango' Series
Feng Shui and the Tango, The Dance of Design
Feng Shui and the Tango, The Essential Chapters
25th Anniversary Edition
FS&T Prosperity Lessons
FS&T Happiness Lessons
The Dream Desk Quiz
The Clutter Bug's Emergency Handbook

Find their books and documentaries at:
www.WineCountryInShorts.com

www.ingramcontent.com/pod-product-compliance
Lightning Source LLC
LaVergne TN
LVHW012024060526
838201LV00061B/4454